DEMAND DRIVEN!

Six Steps to Creating an Ecosystem of Demand for Your Business

DEMAND DRIVEN!

Six Steps to Creating an Ecosystem of Demand for Your Business

Bo Manning
Chris Thorne

McGraw-Hill

New York Chicago San Francisco Lisbon London
Madrid Mexico City Milan New Delhi San Juan
Seoul Singapore Sydney Toronto

The **McGraw·Hill** *Companies*

1 2 3 4 5 6 7 8 9 0 DOC/DOC 0 9 8 7 6 5 4 3 2

ISBN 0-07-158970-8

This publication is designed to provide accurate and authoritative information in regard to the subject matter covered. It is sold with the understanding that neither the author nor the publisher is engaged in rendering legal, accounting, or other professional service. If legal advice or other expert assistance is required, the services of a competent professional person should be sought.

> —*From a Declaration of Principles jointly*
> *adopted by a Committee of the American Bar*
> *Association and a Committee of Publishers*

McGraw-Hill books are available at special quantity discounts to use as premiums and sales promotions, or for use in corporate training programs. For more information, please write to the Director of Special Sales, McGraw-Hill, Two Penn Plaza, New York, NY 10121. Or contact your local bookstore.

This book is printed on recycled, acid-free paper containing a minimum of 50% recycled de-inked fiber.

Contents

Contents

Preface

It's not to difficult to intuitively grasp the concept of "demand driven." In fact, the sense of it is very appealing—focusing your company strategy toward fulfilling the demands of your customers means you're more likely to get the business you're seeking. But there is a lot to doing this and to making the connection with those customers so you can deliver what they want. The purpose of this book is to help you better understand how to do that.

This book emphasizes learning how to use IT, the Internet, and other business partners to profitably meet customer demands. It further suggests using these tools to shape demand, not to manipulate customers, but to help customers understand their needs and perceive your offerings as appropriate to those needs. Being demand driven ultimately means taking advantage of all the tools at your disposal to run an operation that can most effectively, efficiently, and profitably build, maintain, and grow mutually beneficial relationships with customers.

In a manner of speaking, what you will learn in this book is not new. You'll find examples and recommendations for being creative in productive development, modifying current offerings to appeal to new customer groups, and figuring out how to continuously reinvent your business. What's new is using IT, the Internet, and other tools to do this in a more informed and strategic manner.

One of the concepts we introduce is the idea of the "customer ecosystem." An ecosystem takes in all the components in the environment and suggests their interrelationships and mutual dependencies. A customer ecosystem suggests a similar set of interrelationships and dependencies to create continuing demand for products and services from a business. We teach you how to understand and map your customer ecosystem, with special emphasis on market processes—the ongoing and evolving relationships among the components of this ecosystem. You'll see how to view customers as the center of the ecosystem and the importance of focusing on the customers' experience and their relationship not only with the company but with all elements of the value chain.

In understanding the customer ecosystem, we look at three groups of customers. Collaborative customers are those who willingly work with their suppliers to exchange information and develop new products and services. Activist customers are those who seek a high level of control in their relationship with suppliers. Such customers provide detailed specifications to suppliers for their products and services—automotive manufacturers are just one example of such customers. Finally, there are passive customers. Such customers are less interested in a relationship with suppliers than in having their needs filled efficiently and effectively. In learning to manage the customer ecosystem, you'll learn how to deal with these different groups of customers.

Further, you'll learn how to identify and benefit from partners in the customer ecosystem to better meet customer demand—partners such as members of the finance community, insurance companies, and distributors. You'll learn how to use technology to facilitate these relationships and how they may evolve and change through time to better meet customer needs. While this is conceptual in nature, we include numerous examples throughout the book to show you how real companies are using these concepts to shape their business strategy.

The book is broken into two parts. Part One, "Six Steps to Building an Ecosystem of Demand for Your Business," looks at the concepts involved in becoming demand driven. Chapters 2 through 7 introduce you to these six steps. Part Two, "Enterprise Demand Management Systems in Practice," takes us from concept to reality. Chapters 8 through 11 give you case studies that demonstrate how companies have taken the principles explained in Part One to build their businesses. The example companies are as diverse as Intrawest (a ski resort company), RBC Capital Markets (the capital markets division of RBC Dain Rauscher), and USFilter (a supplier of water treatment systems). The book concludes with a look at the strategic implications of the ideas in this book and how you can implement the strategies in your business.

Acknowledgments

This book would not have been possible without the constant support and enthusiasm of all the great people at Pivotal Corporation. The authors would like to extend many thanks to Laurie Zettler, Jennifer Walts, Kathy Swift, and Tamara Slater, for coordination of case study research throughout the research project.

The research work completed by Darren Mondor, a graduate student from the Schulich School of Business, is integral to this book. We wish him best of luck in his new role as a systems architect.

We also thank Alexandra Campbell of the Schulich School of Business for her insight and perspective on the critical challenge of customer experience.

Special thanks go to Kirk Herrington for his contribution to the information architecture perspectives in the book, and also to David Kohar for his contribution to the concepts of business impact of demand management.

Chris Thorne would like to thank his special personal supporter, Kim Cassidy Thorne, for enduring the abstracted monologues that did not always crystallize into coherent ideas. He would also like to thank the fine leadership of Unleash Corporation, Larry Kistner and Rick Vyrostko, for their support and patience during this project.

Part 1

Six Steps to Creating an Ecosystem of Demand for Your Business

1

Becoming
Demand Driven

Markets, customers, and distribution channels are increasingly complex and volatile. Searching for answers, companies have embraced new technologies, such as e-business and customer relationship management systems that promise to solve their market and customer challenges and make them more competitive. Yet, these widely hyped and widely adopted technologies have not lived up to their promises. Why not? Because the companies implementing them are not demand driven.

Most companies, even progressive companies aggressively adopting the latest technologies, are still trying to create and meet demand for their products simply by marketing and communicating directly with large groups of potential customers. This is good and important. However, this approach to meeting demand is no longer adequate. It has four problems.

Problem #1: Traditional Business Strategies Underestimate "Indirect Demand"

There are dozens of additional markets full of potential demand that companies are ignoring because they are not able to reach the customers in these markets directly. In effect, there is a world of "indirect demand" waiting to be tapped by savvy organizations. Being demand driven means focusing your organization on meeting both direct demand and the powerful untapped reservoir of indirect demand. It means organizing the marketing and sales and IT infrastructure of your company in such a way that you satisfy both direct demand for your products by your traditional customers and indirect demand. This means communicating and selling your products indirectly through partners to customers who have never heard of your organization.

You already know how to satisfy direct demand for your products or services. Your company has been organized to achieve this goal. This book explains how to become fully demand driven by satisfying indirect demand as well. The secret to tapping indirect demand is the creative use of your IT infrastructure, the Internet, and your business partners to communicate indirectly with many more customers and markets than your organization is currently reaching.

To understand the power of indirect demand, consider the fact that the value of certain products is realized only when they are used with other products. This has given rise to a whole industry of "solution-selling" technology companies. IBM transformed itself from a hardware company into IBM Global Services, tapping into the widely held belief that "you can't go wrong buying IBM." When it became manufacturer agnostic for the technology solutions, it tapped into the indirect demand for many other kinds of products and services that it had previously locked itself out of.

Most organizations today are not tapping into the vast opportunities waiting for them in the form of indirect demand. They are still fixated on internal structure, supply chains, and customer relationship management (CRM). To meet indirect demand, they need to be more flexible and adaptive to the customer and market, without becoming totally meaningless to customers.

The problem with most businesses is that they have no idea that indirect demand is out there waiting for them to exploit it. Consider the technology company that provides emergency backup services for computer networks, called "high-availability" solutions. A high-availability solution ensures that your Web site, accounting system, or manufacturing system do not fail if there is some sort of network or computing problem. Companies that purchase it are buying the assurance that critical information is not lost in the event of any kind of disaster or even minor technical outage. The companies that sell this kind of equipment almost always say it requires an "insurance sell." Some savvy companies—demand driven companies—take the next logical step and partner with business loss insurance companies to completely fulfill the customer's real demand, which is to guard against loss or downtime to a critical computer system. Neither the technology company nor the insurance company could satisfy the indirect demand completely, but together they capture revenue that they would never have earned if they had sold their products separately.

Problem #2: Traditional Business Strategies Focus on Mass Marketing or One-to-One Marketing Instead of Doing Both

The nature of demand has shifted. Traditional mass marketing is still effective, but there is now a large pool of customers who cannot be effectively reached by traditional advertising, marketing, and sales techniques. Companies are rapidly adjusting to the fact that Internet technology has stirred a level of activity among customers, partners, and competitors that has never before been possible. Innovative companies like MBNA Bank and Amazon are perfecting one-to-one marketing techniques by customizing offerings to individuals based on sophisticated data stores that can be collected from several sources and acted upon.

MBNA Bank[1] has been able to create unique credit card offerings for individuals and groups through creative partnerships with membership organizations, like associations, college alumni organizations, and other affinity groups. The company has executed a strategy that is incredibly effective to maintain the loyalty of its cardholders.

American Express, in contrast, is less effective on the one-to-one relationship-marketing front. Customers continue to receive offers for charge or credit cards they already hold—a leading complaint of many cardholders! On the other hand, American Express is much more successful at creating new products and offerings to appeal to a mass market. It is a leader in the creation of new credit tools, like micro-payment products and single-use credit cards—in an effort to create a new standard for payments for online purchases. The combination of the two strengths into one company would be the ultimate demand driven financial services company—one that can address your individual needs and one that is not afraid to make its current mass market products obsolete.

Problem #3: Traditional Businesses Haven't Successfully Used Technology to Support Their Business Strategy

Companies today compete in three main ways: they try to achieve the lowest cost of production, they try to have the best products, or they try to build relationships with customers. Prevailing wisdom is to focus on just one of these three.

To deal with the customer relationship challenge, most companies have implemented some form of customer relationship management system.

Unfortunately, almost 60% of them have found that they were unsuccessful in achieving the level of success that they were promised by the software vendors and the business consultants. This is because they do not understand that connecting with markets and customers requires a change in the way that they think about markets and technology.

Implementing technology for managing customers has created many, many problems for businesses because most companies have expected the technology itself to solve their challenge of building a better business. They implemented a customer relationship management system in the sales group and let the marketing and customer service groups use different processes and different information systems and work from a different customer database. Not only are different systems in use, different goals are at work in the business as well: the marketing group's sole purpose is to create leads, the sales group may have a key account management strategy in place, and the customer support group is trying reduce the amount of time it takes to solve a customer problem.

For example, Wall Street analysts told one software company to achieve 60% of revenue from new customer sales. If they don't report progress toward that goal on a quarterly basis, their stock price declines rapidly. Understandably, they focus their limited resources on automating the sales function to the exclusion of all other customer relationship functions. They also have teams of consultants and a whole customer support organization that has specific goals for solving business problems. What occurs, of course, is that each separate department employs a technology to solve its own problem, rather than work toward the overall strategic objective of both reaching overall sales goals and gaining 60% of their business from new customers. So their reputation for maintaining relationships and solving customer problems is somewhat lacking. Interestingly, increased customer defections are causing them to have more difficulty reaching Wall Street's overall revenue goal, but less difficulty in reaching the target of 60% new customers.

Problem #4: Traditional Business Strategies Can't Keep Up with Constant Change and Complexity in Markets and Customers

Nobody said it would be easy, but doesn't it look like markets and customers just keep getting more difficult to understand and their demands more difficult to manage?

Armed with more information and able to connect to a broader range of "virtual" distributors and traditional competitors that happen to be a world away, your customers—the ones that you think you "own"—are getting advice from other customers and service from other suppliers that you are not even aware of.

Just because the "dot-com" era is over doesn't mean that the threat of new competitors arising from nowhere is over. In fact, this is probably the most dangerous period for companies, as they face much more credible new competitors entering their markets. These new competitors come from two distinct angles: the large multinational corporation that keeps sprawling into areas that its customers feel are related and the small boutique operated by your own former employees that can provide specialized service for your highest-value customers.

What Does It Mean to Be Demand Driven?

Being demand driven means tapping indirect demand by smart use of IT, the Internet, and business partners. It means creating demand with both old mass marketing tools and new one-to-one marketing tools and understanding how these two approaches work together.

This sounds complex and hard to do. It is much simpler to understand and implement, however, if you change the way you think about your customers. While most people recognize that today's customer is more connected, informed, and discerning than ever in the past, few have been able to fully appreciate the implications of the new structure of demand relationships at work today.

Demand, in a purely economic sense, is the sum of individual purchases in a national or international market economy. From this perspective, demand is a result of a whole series of individual transactions. Consumer demand is the collective need or desire for a good or service. demand driven companies understand both the industry level of demand as well as the individual level. They create demand, directly and indirectly, by trying to forge a standard, or set of rules, that will govern the way a family of products is used in a marketplace.

Demand Driven Means Continually Changing Your Mix of Products and Services

In today's economy, market demand is mostly unpredictable. The impact of media and communications has created a powerful consumer, while rapid shifts in market situations have caused similarly rapid changes in demand for goods in the business-to-business sector.

We believe that, in order to compete effectively in this environment, companies must be willing both to create market demand and to respond to market demand. If the best that you can hope for is continuous change, the best response is to foster continuous change in how you deal with the market. The challenge is to be willing to render leading products obsolete by introducing replacement products.

In any ecosystem, diversity improves the survival success of ecosystem inhabitants, whether they are species or products. In Hawaii, because of centuries of isolation, over 88% of native birds and 10% of native plants were unable to defend themselves and disappeared after the introduction of rats, pigs, goats, and mongooses. This is the kind of lesson that General Electric had in mind when it encouraged existing business units to come up with a new e-business initiative called "Destroy-Your-Business.com."[2] Meaningful diversity is not just new versions and enhancements of the old. It is the recognition that markets change, so you might as well be the one making the changes.

Adaptation has also been long about how to complement or compete with other companies simultaneously. For USFilter, one of the world's largest wastewater treatment companies, being adaptive means combining products from several companies and putting them under one roof. Adapting a combination of products and services to each individual client location enables USFilter to address specific treatment needs for individual customers. While some customers of USFilter prefer to manage the specifics of wastewater treatment, others are more hands-off and want USFilter to provide these services. In recent years, USFilter has grown its capability to provide outsourced service. Thus, it has adapted its core business of managing wastewater to customer demand for both hands-on clients and those who want to outsource.

Demand Driven Means Distributing Your Business Capabilities to Partners, Customers, and Employees

Becoming demand driven means linking your business to customers, partners, and employees through technology—both Internet technology and more traditional information systems, as well as training, both face-to-face and distance learning. The key is to use information systems and training strategically to generate new business. "Upselling," for example, is a business capability that McDonald's has used to create higher profit margins than most of its competitors. McDonald's has extended its franchise and its ability to upsell through a combination of information systems and training that reminds even the newest employee to always ask, "Do you want to supersize that?" McDonald's franchisee partners must buy into both the training and the technology from the McDonald's organization, effectively distributing this upselling capability throughout the network of franchisees within the chain. Distributed capabilities are a way to place critical skills in the hands of the many people who touch the customer—phone reps, business partners, salespeople, Web sites, partner Web sites, etc.

Distributing business capabilities and creating indirect relationships with customers in the Internet-enabled economy is much easier and much more valuable because the emergence of new Web- and technology-based connections. An example comes from RBC Dain Rauscher, one of many dynamic, competitive investment banks that have survived and thrived in the good, the bad, and the ugly times of the recent economy. As a much smaller player than the powerhouses of investment banking like Merrill Lynch or Morgan Stanley Dean Witter, RBC Dain Rauscher wisely chooses not to directly compete with the bigger investment players. Instead it has invested heavily in enabling its staff with knowledge management technology to create and distribute their stock analysts' recommendations, leveraging their key skills in research and client management. RBC Dain Rauscher creates consistency within its sales force by linking research and customer relationship through technology. The customer ecosystem in RBC Dain Rauscher's world exists primarily among three critical parties: the portfolio manager who makes the recommendation for a particular security, the salesperson who builds the relationship, and the analyst who influences the portfolio manager's perceptions and the trader who makes the transaction happen.

Demand Driven Means Connected to Indirect Demand Through Technology, Partners, and Solutions

Even though most companies today have a range of communications and information technology tools transmitting information between themselves and their customers, the idea of connection to the sources of indirect demand is evolving rapidly. Connecting with indirect demand requires connection through the established and emerging standards of Internet technology in a physical sense. In a metaphorical sense, connecting with demand means understanding the different pockets where new sources of demand can emerge.

Being connected to demand today requires use of many kinds of connections at once. Following the downturn in the dot-com economy, a glut of used computing equipment became available on the market. Many existing companies and some new ones found that it was good business to buy the high-quality notebook computers and other hardware equipment from leasing companies to resell them used to consumers. In the past, this kind of company may have had a few avenues to reach their customers: newspaper, magazine, and direct mail. Today, these avenues of mass marketing are still important, but the technology angle adds complexity. First of all, a commerce-enabled Web site is necessary to sell directly to the individuals who find the companies. Second, and perhaps more important, participation in major marketplaces for used computing equipment, the most prominent being eBay, enables the companies to be connected to the locations where their customers are looking for equipment. Third, heavy usage of e-mail newsletters to other used equipment sellers enables a collective approach for many players to fulfill demand for a specific product, even if it is through one of their competitors.

Take the example of Wet Ones, the moistened antibacterial wipe from Playtex Products, as an example of how companies can connect with indirect demand through solutions. Wet Ones, was an extension of the basic concept of the moistened towelette common in fast food restaurants. Playtex and other companies saw that the convenience of the combination of a cleaning liquid and a paper towel could be extended to numerous other products like Clorox bleach for cleaning and disinfecting or Armor-All for cleaning and shining car interiors. There are countless examples of how a product from one company can be combined in a "solution" with a product from another company to connect to the indirect demand for products that may even be your competition. Solving customer problems requires imagination and insight beyond the typical capability of product manufacturing.

Connections among customers, employees, suppliers, and other customer ecosystem participants are becoming increasingly data-intensive. Information standards for communicating business data are becoming much more open. In the past, database standards for computers, such as those for mainframe computers, were not designed to be easily accessible and adopted by a broad market. As the current wave of change toward more open technology standards continues, it will become much easier for the majority of companies to utilize and adopt data communication standards like the Sun Microsystems-backed Java 2 Enterprise Edition or the Microsoft-backed .NET standard. It is already important to be connected within the boundaries of your company; what is becoming easier and important is fluid connections outside those boundaries.

Intrawest: A Demand Driven Company

Intrawest Corporation operates 16 of the most prestigious recreational sports properties in North America and Europe. Many of its resort locations are household names, like Stratton in Vermont, Copper Mountain in Colorado, and

Whistler Blackcomb in British Columbia. Traditionally their business has been winter sports, like skiing and snowboarding. As the proprietor of the physical property of a ski hill, it would seem that Intrawest has unique and valuable assets that consumers (of a certain nature) will search out—implying, of course, that it is a likely candidate to be supply-driven company.

In practice, however, it is far from being supply-driven. Intrawest is faced with several factors that force it to be much more proactive than its competitors may be. Its approach to the customer and the broader market simultaneously makes it a demand driven company.

First of all, the managers have a keen understanding of all the different factors that affect their customers' recreation decisions. Their perception of what goes on in the customer ecosystem includes the many short-term competitors—like other ski resorts and perhaps other winter sports activities—and the competing long-term threats, like a decrease in the number of people who know how to ski or snowboard. Their perception of the customer ecosystem also includes the threat from entertainment activities in general, wherein companies like Disney set the standard for all resort operators to meet.

Adaptation

Recognizing the challenge of the many competing recreational activities is one thing, but doing something about it is another. Intrawest is heavily focused on getting the right properties—some of the best on the market—and ensuring that the quality of the physical terrain is matched by high-quality hotel and residence facilities. Intrawest, like most businesses, needs to cope with an aging customer. Adaptation to this inevitability takes several forms. For example, Intrawest provides more than just the means to go vertically up and down a hill: it provides the option to buy real estate at a favorite resort property; it provides summer activities such as golf; its resorts are fully stocked with non-skiing activities like restaurants, spas, and theaters; and it is increasingly diversifying into non-skiing activities by creating golf locations in southern locales like Florida.

Forcing Change on the Market

Most ski operators have traditionally held a "one person, one pass" policy. Intrawest has found it more effective to sacrifice short-term revenue in order to ensure a long-term market. A few years ago, Intrawest pioneered the Parent Pass that could be shared by two parents, provided that a child accompanied the parent. From Intrawest's vantage point, this will help populate the future of the ski market.

Build Technology in Close Concert with Strategy

First-class experience in a hospitality setting is often about the "little things." For example, if you order a special meal on an airplane, you expect to receive it. Intrawest recently launched a vacation planning system that is intended to iron out all the "little things" before guests arrive at their resorts. The vacation planner is intended to help the customer create a vacation experience that is fully thought out: if ski passes are needed, they can be ordered ahead of time; if lessons are needed, they too can be ordered ahead; if a spa package is desired ... well, you get the picture. This technology was not an afterthought or a nice-to-have feature.

Distribute Capabilities to Customers, Employees, Partners, and Suppliers

The customer ecosystem for a vacation resort includes a wide range of people; often the most visible relationship is between customers and employees. The vacation planning system is integrated with many other systems, including the reservation system, so it ensures that employees have the ability to understand the full scope of each customer's needs. Other companies that supply services in an Intrawest resort village may be tied into the technology systems to ensure that they provide the capabilities that create the right experience for resort guests.

Connected with Demand ...

Finally, Intrawest connects with demand through traditional travel agencies, as well as its own vacation planning Web sites. Through its real estate division, it connects with the demand for property through real estate agents. It also connects with some indirect pockets of demand through personal relationships. Whistler Blackcomb, one of its premiere resorts, has a relationship with Australia to recruit resort employees. This connection also provides a relationship with a segment of patrons who come to work and ski—something of a rite of passage for Australian students to come ski in North America for a year. This approach has built demand and a reputation for Intrawest locations as being an exciting place for college students from around the world.

Becoming Demand Driven

What are the steps involved in becoming demand driven?

Step 1. Uncover the dynamics of customer experience by mapping your customer ecosystem. The first section of the book will help you understand your customer ecosystem. Market and consumer demand can come from a variety of sources; you have the choice of being prepared for change (or not) or influencing change (or not). This chapter will look at the dynamics of customer ecosystem relationships and the pockets of indirect demand that are within your reach.

First, we will examine the nature of customer ecosystems facing organizations today and how they have evolved due to converging technologies and particularly the Internet into a complex, constantly changing system. Understanding this will help you understand your customers better. We will also develop an approach to mapping your customer ecosystem so that you can increase its effectiveness at directing demand to your organization.

Step 2. Partner with other companies in your ecosystem. We explore how alliances and partners are changing in a complex network environment. Key principles are illustrated by drawing on examples from industry leaders who have used demand driven partnering principles to their advantage.

Step 3. Build adaptive strategies to create and respond to customer demand. In an interconnected economy, forces of demand must be both stoked and harnessed simultaneously. Creation of new demand is risky and can cost substantial time and expense to companies, but unquestionably still necessary to create new business opportunities. Companies must make the investment to create new demand but must also hedge their bets to respond to existing demand if they are to survive. We explore the combinations of strategies that best match the needs of the customers in your ecosystem.

Step 4. Take stock of technology tools for the ecosystem. Existing effectively in a customer ecosystem requires that you have technology that meshes with the requirements of the customer ecosystem. Customer relationship management software is often a good start, but it is not enough, and often has not been implemented properly. Typically, what remains after a company has implemented CRM is the coordination and integration of these building blocks under the customer ecosystem concept, using open computing technologies. Technology infrastructure that can help provide a basis for fertilizing a customer ecosystem includes a range of software solutions designed to help marketing, sales, customer service, interactive selling, and partner management.

Step 5. Turn business processes into ecosystem capabilities. Customer interaction capabilities include personalizion, transaction, service, and fulfillment. We look at these capabilities as the skills and technology that win the battle for short-term market share.

Positioning capabilities enable companies to respond to customers, competitors, and other ecosystem stimuli. The generic positioning capabilities that companies need to create, manage, and distribute throughout their customer ecosystem are adapt, influence, engage, and understand. These capabilities are the skills and technology that win the battle for long-term mind share. The specific capabilities include many of the traditional marketing functions, such as sales, marketing communications, and promotions that are increasingly carried out by people outside of the traditional marketing organization.

Step 6. Synchronize your customer ecosystem and supply chain. If the customer ecosystem and the supply chain concepts are like the left and right hemispheres of the brain, the secret of success is to utilize the benefits of each side to improve the other. In essence, companies need to learn to adopt flexible, yet rigorous approaches to responding to demand in the supply chain, while simultaneously building context and structure into predicting the behavior of the customer ecosystem.

In order to do this, we outline how companies can:

◆ Respond or plan for adaptation of the supply chain
◆ Infuse a supply chain with a more flexible structure
◆ Predict demand through the demand community more rigorously
◆ Anticipate and manipulate ecosystem behavior more effectively.

Notes

1. Frederick F. Reichheld, *Loyalty Rules! How Today's Leaders Build Lasting Relationships*, Harvard Business School Press, 2001.
2. Richard T. Pascale, Mark Millemann, and Linda Gioja, *Surfing the Edge of Chaos*, Random House/Crown, 2000.

2

Step 1: Understand Customer Demand by Mapping Your Customer Ecosystem

Traditional telephones, digital wireless phones, and the Internet are the physical components of new types of social connections in a world of people in contact like never before—through e-mail and chat, through telecommunications tools, and through traditional and converging media of television, radio, Internet, and print.

In business, this complex maze of connections has allowed the emergence of more mutually dependent relationships between businesses and consumers that take the form of a "customer ecosystem." In nature, an ecosystem is a complex grouping of mutually dependent flora, fauna, insects, and microorganisms. A customer ecosystem is a complex grouping of companies and customers, suppliers, and partners that gain mutual benefit from one another.

The customer ecosystem metaphor helps us to understand our core concept of what it means to be demand driven: *the interaction of companies and individuals creates demand (directly and indirectly) for products and services.* Most important, the customer ecosystem metaphor helps us focus on the *process* of the market rather than the *state*. That is, we should be as concerned with the flows of information, influence, and economic impact within an ecosystem as we are with the current situation in terms of market share or price level or any one of a dozen other measurements.

15

Within the complex ecosystem of markets and customers, the primary inhabitants—the buyer and the supplier—and many new and emerging supporting participants will shift the focus and nature of their roles. Constantly, the central activity in a market shifts from supplier to customer and back again. It becomes difficult to determine if either supplier or customer is the dominant species in the ecosystem. For example, in automotive manufacturing, traditionally companies like Ford and Toyota set many elements of the business relationship, including terms, product design, and communications standards for their suppliers, because they have control of the end product and are significantly larger than their suppliers.

In a demand driven customer ecosystem, market activities that are traditionally supplier-driven interactions—like relationship investment, joint product or service development, market communications and influence, logistics, and transaction communications—are undertaken and controlled by the buyer rather than the supplier. This happens not just in situations where there is an imbalance of power in favor of the buyer; it can easily occur when customers are much smaller than their suppliers.

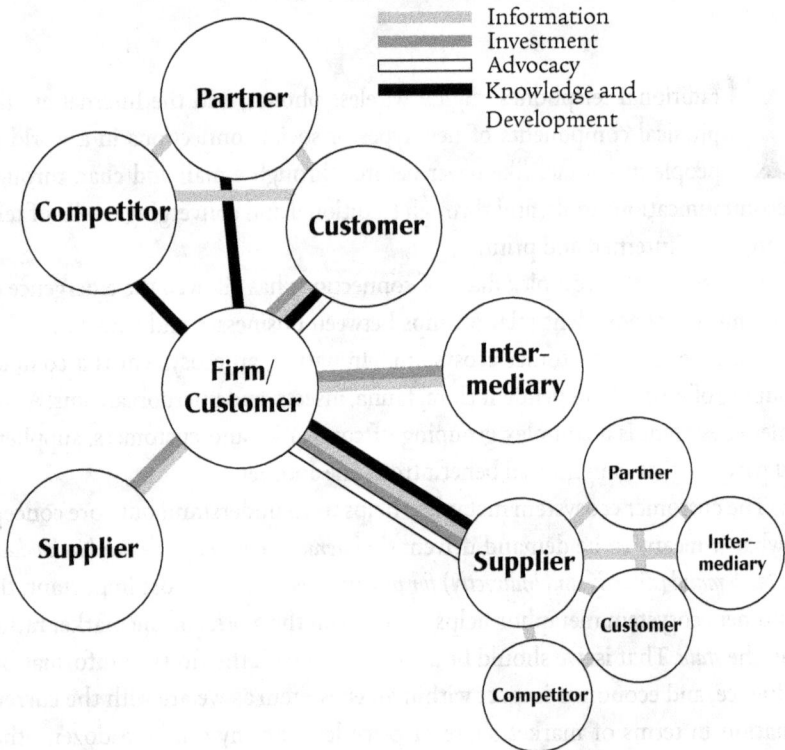

Figure 2-1. Mapping the customer ecosystem

Ecosystems Deal with the Process of the Market, Not the State

Customer ecosystems are always in flux. With many players and many actions, communications, influences, and activities occurring, the constant interactions and adjustments are what are important.

Companies should be concerned with a range of *flows* in the ecosystem that affect the relationship among their business, their customers, and other ecosystem participants. Information, intellectual capital, investment, and economic influence shift the balance of power from supplier to customer in dynamic flows. In a customer ecosystem, the flows between supplier and customer are as follows:

♦ **The flow of information for advocacy and influence.** Communications designed to influence buying behavior are the traditional process of a market. In a customer ecosystem, influence can originate from any of the major players or from the expanding variety of other participants. For example, one of the most powerful communications forces for resort owner Intrawest is its customers communicating with one another about ski hill conditions, new programs for children, and other factors that generate demand from the customers' perspective.

♦ **The flow of ideas for new products and services.** Participants in an ecosystem develop products, services, or experiences that are the reason and sometimes the vehicle for commerce. Traditional markets feature the development of products and services by the supplier to sell to potential buyers. In contrast, evolving customer ecosystems will frequently involve "co-development" of products, services, or experiences. Thus, the process of the market involves mutual dependency and complementarities that blur the roles of buyer versus supplier or supplier versus intermediary. For example, Procter & Gamble product teams participate with their suppliers, like enzyme manufacturer Novozymes, to improve the products that they purchase. While the enzyme manufacturer produces a key ingredient for Procter & Gamble, responsibility for product development is shared, improved as a result of complementarities.

♦ **The flow of investment for commitment and connection.** Relationship investment to build connection traditionally flows from supplier to buyers. For example, American Express supplies financial services to consumers worldwide. It builds connections and relationships with customers by investing in communications tools, like Web sites, account statements, and call centers to make this more convenient for its card members. The card members, however, also invest in the relationship through sharing information about their investment plans and investment goals. This investment of time and commitment related to personal information creates a closer connection, one of trust and expected value.

◆ **The flow and amplification of revenue to ecosystem participants.** The economics and process of other customer ecosystems are embedded within another ecosystem. USFilter supplies municipal and commercial water filtration systems; cities, towns, and businesses are its core customers. The viability of its customer relationships is dependent on the viability of consultants and engineers who advise on water management and specifications for the systems. This is the flow that is most important for influencing indirect demand. We cover this in more detail in Chapter 3.

The Customer at the Center of the Ecosystem

If there is a metaphor that describes the relationship that knowledgeable business and consumer buyers have with suppliers today, it is the metaphor of arranger or conductor. Customers have an increased ability to share control and to collaborate with their vendors or suppliers. They view themselves as capable of organizing goods, services, and experiences for their own ultimate benefit, sourced from many suppliers to suit their particular needs at any given time. This makes customers harder to predict and harder to classify into segments.

The image of the customer as standing in front of the orchestra—first strings, then horns, and then percussion—slightly ahead of the music and part of it, depending on the need and desired outcome. Perhaps it is not as elegant or poetic as that, but many companies seek to provide their customers with the equally poetic "ultimate customer experience." Prediction is the problem today: predicting what a customer values as experience and predicting what role this particular customer wants to play.

Mapping the Customer Experience

What is important to map in the customer ecosystem is how customers experience their role and relationship within the ecosystem. The main things that affect customer experience are advocacy, connection, co-development, and commitment.

In order to map this experience, you must understand the dynamics from the customer's perspective.

Customers understand their value as an asset. Many companies view their customers as an asset, a result of several years of customer loyalty and retention programs. Banks, airlines, book clubs, and a host of other companies use loyalty cards or loyalty programs to attempt to keep customers coming back. To some extent, this has resulted in customers becoming conditioned to understand their worth as an asset.

Programs like Fairmont Hotel's President's Club are built around the guest preference profile. Any Fairmont hotel or resort can instantly know a guest's preferences for his or her stay. This could be a small detail, like a choice of a feather pillow, or something more substantial, like a non-smoking room. Regardless, the guest preference profile makes possible a higher level of personal service. With Fairmont, the excellence is all in the details. In the end, management is confident that these small touches combine to create the luxury experience that will encourage guests to return frequently.

Customers can create products in conjunction with their suppliers. Another core role of the customer in the organization is that of creative force for new offerings. With the rise of mass customization and online personalization capability, it seems obvious that companies can enable their customers to create new combinations of products that meet their needs more exactly. Creation of the exact pair of jeans to match exact measurements and style requirements has been possible for many years from Levi Strauss.[1]

Understanding customers is not simply a data collection exercise or even a data storage and retrieval issue, although many companies tackle the customer knowledge question as though it were. Customers today *need* to contribute to their business relationships. Especially in business markets, customer value will come from mutually finding ways to decrease cost of doing business.

Customers can influence other customers with incredible speed and reach. Among the many things that the Internet has enabled, one of the most important is the creation of a means to interact in a community of like-minded people without the restriction of distance. E-mail, bulletin boards, and chat rooms have helped consumers or business buyers to exchange information about a range of things, not the least of which is information about products and services. In the grand scheme of things, it is obvious that this expands the impact of the vocal minority—those customers who want to speak on your behalf have a greater potential to do so.

The classic example of rapid growth of product adoption through technology is the growth of Hotmail, the free e-mail service. Another example of rapid and amplified influence through technology is the movie *The Blair Witch Project*. Through e-mail and chat rooms, moviegoers told one another about this film, which was positioned as a real documentary. The electronic word of mouth was supplemented by communications from the movies distributor, but primarily it was a word-of-mouth phenomenon.

The Keystone Species: The Collaborative Customer

In nature, the species that can most dramatically affect the balance of an ecosystem is called the *keystone species*. Humans, of course, represent the keystone species in most ecosystems that they affect. In a customer ecosystem, the keystone species will vary based on the breadth of control, influence, and involvement the customer wishes.

Customers are more willing and able to control the buyer-supplier relationship or to be active in their relationship with their suppliers. Each of the roles above may be part of that relationship, making it therefore much more necessary for the vendor to dynamically profile this behavior.

In a customer ecosystem, we have identified three major subspecies of customer, each varying in their degree of control over their customer experience.

The Collaborative Customer

Increasingly, customers are able and willing to share in the control of the relationship with their suppliers. A high proportion of relationships in the business-to-business sector are evolving to this nature. Business buyers like Procter & Gamble and their suppliers, such as Novozymes, collaborate on a huge range of issues. Joint investment in systems that connect both companies, a willingness to share information and learn from it, and joint projects and problem solving characterize the collaborative customer relationship. Table 2-1 summarizes some characteristics of this type of customer.

Shared control between customer and supplier involves an exchange of information on the wants and desires of the customer along with the basics of offerings by the supplier. In many ways this is the ideal type of customer orientation for one-to-one marketing to work.

Consumer markets are increasingly of this type. The tourism industry, for example, traditionally was led by the travel agent intermediary. Today, the opportunities for the customer to share control of the relationship abound; research is conducted by the consumer, price shopping may be done by an automated Internet shopping service, but the relationship with a travel agent is valued for the knowledge and expertise and an ability to coordinate many different requirements, such as flight times, connections, and hotel reservations.

In the automotive sector, parts suppliers are increasingly expected to provide

Relationship Risk and Investment	Commitment flows from supplier to customer and vice versa. Risk may be shared; investment in the relationship is mutual.
Knowledge Capital and Shared Development	Moderate to high level of knowledge on the part of the customer. Strong potential for sharing knowledge and jointly creating new products.
Advocacy	Moderate to high potential for customer to influence others on the supplier's behalf.
Information Flow and Connection	Two-way flow of information from supplier to customers (interaction in a variety of media).

Table 2-1. Characteristics of the collaborative customer

expertise in the development and engineering of products. In order to maintain a contract with one of the global automotive manufacturers, contributing to a design that lowers cost of production or ensures faster manufacturing cycle time is simply expected as part of the relationship.

The Activist Customer

In some circumstances, customers seek a high level of control of the business customer experience. In many industrial markets, this may be the most common relationship between the leading auto manufacturers and their suppliers. Manufacturers that act as customers set the specifications, delivery requirements and cost parameters, and their suppliers meet these terms. Table 2-2 lists characteristics of the activist customer.

Computer users often fall into this category as well, but from a slightly different perspective. The degree of activism, for example, of Apple Macintosh users is not the result of economic power, as in the case of auto manufacturers and their suppliers. It is more the result of enthusiasm and connectedness. Mac users participate in user groups and avidly assist Apple with new development and with product evangelism. Their participation as a community and their loyalty to the Mac product platform are impressive.

Wouldn't all companies want the activist customer? That depends. Sometimes activist customers control the options of the suppliers, reducing them and placing the suppliers at strategic risk. In the Apple example, the extreme loyalty and commitment of their customers gave Apple a false impression of its control of the market, ultimately blindsiding the company to the changes beyond its customers' control.

Relationship Risk and Investment	The supplier may be selected from many capable of fulfilling the specific needs; risk is borne by the supplier and not shared.
Knowledge Capital and Shared Development	High level of knowledge on the part of the customer and high willingness to become more knowledgeable make it likely that customer will contribute to new products or services.
Advocacy	Customer is capable of a high level of influence on the success of the supplier and the markets that the customer builds for the supplier.
Information Flow and Connection	Initiating the two-way flow of information between supplier and customer, customer invests to improve the flow of data to ensure extensive communication with the supplier.

Table 2-2. Characteristics of the activist customer

The Passive Customer

A passive customer is primarily one who has a low level of involvement with his or her customer experience. Being passive typically has a negative connotation, generally implying lazy or uninterested. However, there are still many situations where consumers or business customers are not particularly interested in a "relationship."

As one can imagine, the situations where customers are legitimately passive are not as numerous today as they were pre-Information Age. Few customers of the funeral home industry, for example, will have a great deal of willingness to learn or become better consumers of funeral services.

The passive stance of customers does not imply that they do not want more information or better service to make the relationship more effective. As in other roles, customers taking a passive consumer stance also want visibility into the status of orders and visibility into the status of customer service problems; just don't expect that more information will earn corresponding investment or commitment from your customers.

Reducing the glut of data aimed at the buyer and delivering the right value-added information can provide value by ensuring that the relationship is not complicated by unnecessary, extraneous data.

Relationship Risk and Investment	Customer does not tend to be particularly loyal, at least not to the degree that investment in the relationship will be primarily from the customer.
Knowledge Capital and Shared Development	Customer shows low willingness to become more knowledgeable or to participate in the development of new products or solutions.
Advocacy	Customer's low level of knowledge makes it unlikely that the company can harness or stimulate advocacy.
Information Flow and Connection	Primarily, flow of information is one way, from supplier to customers (traditional outbound marketing communication).

Table 2-3. Characteristics of the passive customer

How Should Businesses Deal with the Dynamics of Demand in a Customer Ecosystem?

Direct demand and indirect demand work together in a customer ecosystem. The next chapter will explain more fully the dynamics of how indirect demand supports the customer ecosystem.

Understand That Customer Experience Drives the Ecosystem

At the heart of the ecosystem is a customer. In today's communications-, media-, and technology-dominated world, customers of all stripes can hold whatever degree of control they want. They can closely participate in product development or highly influence the flow of information among organizations, customers, and partners. Not all customers desire more relationship with their suppliers, so it is critical not to overestimate or overinvest in the tools, technologies, and techniques of customer intimacy.

Determine How You Want to Share Control of Customer Experience

It may or may not be valuable for a company to build increased relationship with customers and collaboration with customers may not be possible or even desirable. Can you influence your customers to support product development, to build your market, to share information, or to create connection?

Note

1. As documented in the groundbreaking article by B. Joseph Pine II, Don Peppers, and Martha Rogers, "Do You Want to Keep Your Customers Forever?," *Harvard Business Review*, March-April 1995, p. 108.

3

Step 2: Leverage Ecosystem Partners to Take Advantage of Indirect Demand

The more forms of partnering you have at your disposal, the better off your entire ecosystem is going to be. Lasting direct and indirect demand will be generated as a result of a reinforcing network of partners. Indirect demand is the demand for the products and services, financing, etc. that support your core product or service.

Traditionally, companies have used partners for extending reach into new markets for the development of distribution. Partners in a customer ecosystem may provide a simple distribution function, but they also extend the value of their offerings by partnering with ecosystem leaders. demand driven companies add value not just to their own products and services but to their partners' products as well, to enhance the health of the whole ecosystem. Indirect demand works to build an industry rather than just a market.

Building Indirect Demand

Alliances and partners help to create the ecosystem of demand for your products, services, or experience by helping to build stable bonds between customers and the use of your products, even when your organization has no direct contact with these customers. Often your partners build your ecosystem by sharing information and adopting common business standards, shared knowledge, and agreement among partners within the ecosystem. Yet, even knowing the importance of interrelationships, many companies continue to struggle with the creation of shared applications and communications networks that would enable the full potential of their partnerships.

Match Ecosystem Dynamics to the Right Partners

The first challenge for leveraging partners for ecosystem growth and stability is to determine what kind of indirect demand helps partners to thrive and what you can do to provide this to them. Building relationships with partners that are not better off economically as a result of your contact will not build an ecosystem of demand. The fundamental issue is that companies must be able to grow a customer ecosystem overall to capitalize on direct and indirect demand. The first step is understanding deeply the businesses of the partners that can support and grow indirect demand in your customer ecosystem.

Five Types of Partners in a Customer Ecosystem

Traditional business partnerships provide for distribution of a supplier's product at the retail level. The wholesaler collects a range of goods and provides warehousing and product assortment functions to its downstream partner, the retailer. The retailer, in turn, provides a supplier with a window on the world, so that consumers can purchase their products. By and large, many mature traditional industries, especially food and consumer products, continue to work well within this framework.

For the demand driven organization, the combinations of partners in a customer ecosystem provide much more than just distribution. With complex products and services, many more functions than just location and assortment must be provided. The types of partner found in various customer ecosystems are integrator, syndicator, aggregator, educator, and underwriter (explained below). One of the toughest parts of creating an ecosystem of demand is to figure out how partners are motivated to build demand. Each of these partner types is motivated differently, because their business structures are different.

Integrators. Integrators incorporate your product or service within another service or product (thus modifying it) to build collective demand. Integrators help improve the value of a product. They are able to capture value in the demand ecosystem through fees or service charges.

Incentives for integrators must align with their ability to generate revenue. Because revenue is typically generated through fees, incentives must improve their ability to generate margin or total volume of fees. Supporting the skill of an integrator through training is a tried-and-true approach because it may enable them to collect new types of fees or higher levels of fees for their services.

Integrators exist in many industries. Systems integrators like IBM in software, telecommunications, and other technical markets are most prominent. Engineering firms like Fluor Daniel integrate construction, architecture, urban planning, and other services for municipalities and other government bodies. World Sports Distribution Network, a small distributor of golf-related products that customizes apparel and golf equipment as well as providing inventory and order management services for golf pro shops, qualifies as an integrator as well. Customization is another common form of integration. Custom cars, custom golf clubs, etc., make money not by volume but by the added value of the modifications to the standard product.

Syndicators. Syndicators package, bundle, and resell your product or service and thus distribute it to a broader market. Syndicating information online is an increasingly viable business strategy. A syndicator can be both a producer and a demand development partner at the same time, particularly when it comes to the syndication of information.

Incentives for syndicators also must align with their ability to earn revenue, but in a different way from the integrator—much more dependent on volume than on services, although services may have some role in their business model.

CBS MarketWatch is a successful producer and syndicator of financial information. It creates financial information through the CBS news-gathering infrastructure for its own direct customers, but also distributes the content, including both written and Web-broadcast, through a range of other organizations, like Yahoo and other portal sites that repackage content. This develops demand for both CBS MarketWatch and its partner organizations through the provision of information in generic and specialized formats.

Aggregators. Aggregators provide a broad access to sources of demand by collecting products or services that together give value because of their proximity with one another. This is differentiated from syndication by focus as much as anything: syndicators focus on collecting and packaging products, while aggregators focus on collecting buyers and may or may not package or bundle products. Emerging in importance are online demand access providers like marketplaces and exchanges. More traditional demand aggregators include resellers and retailers, whose job it is to access customers. From a demand strategy point of view, aggregators are more oriented to the interception of demand than to the creation of demand.

Many forms of demand aggregators exist: many, many variations on the theme thrive online and in traditional forms! In the online world, portals like Yahoo! try to aggregate demand and provide a location for product companies to sell their products. Big box stores, malls, and supermarkets all aggregate demand. The real variation on this theme comes from the ability of the demand aggregator to shift the locus of the demand ecosystem into its favor; that is, to tip the balance of power its way. Aggregators do this through many means—private labeling, education functions, financing: that basically means they provide all the tools of demand development in one spot.

Amazon.com, of course, is a demand aggregator. It's a long way from just being a bookseller: its use of technology to personalize and respond to customers' interests has launched it beyond the capabilities of traditional retailers. The collection of products that it sells has certainly expanded its reach into new pockets of demand.

Educators. Educators provide a curriculum for the public and for other ecosystem partners to learn about a product, service, or category. With increasing complexity of products or services, technical education helps to support demand by enabling understanding of the details and requirements for integration.

Is this unique to digital products and services? Digital products such as software and telecommunications services seem to be more complex and specific and thus need specific education. But financial services and other complicated products also need education. The role of education channels in creating demand for such products tends to be less product-specific and more industry-oriented. Financial planners and insurance professionals must be educated by the industry.

Standards form an important part of motivation strategy for education partners. By supporting a standard that transcends a substantial market segment, educators support the demand for specialists like integrators or aggregators, thus creating a revenue opportunity for themselves.

Education also helps to ensure quality and, to some extent, exclusivity, by determining levels of knowledge that the public should both expect and respect.

Even small market segments can support education partners. In the early days of the CRM market (even before it was called CRM), ACT! Certified Trainers provided education to individual salespeople or company sales teams on how to use Symantec's ACT! contact management software. Symantec provided education on customizing or integrating its software directly to its distribution channel, but it also enabled an educator class of partners to help improve end-user knowledge on all the capabilities of its software. By improving the breadth of knowledge, it hoped to ensure continuity in its customer base and thus ensure a more stable level of demand.

Real estate professionals, to look at a non-digital example, are trained and licensed by an industry association to ensure that the quality of the industry is upheld. Education is an industry role because the industry sells a standard product.

Underwriters. There are many kinds of other demand development partners that enable demand from a financial perspective. For examples, demand for automobiles took off in 2001 because of deferred payments rather than product attributes. The ecosystem of demand for cars really depended on the credit providers as much as the manufacturers. And of course today, all major car manufacturers have financial services divisions that facilitate demand for cars. Major department stores have credit cards, either through their own capabilities or through partnerships. It's not just to create demand for the physical product; it's also to capture the potential revenue of the financing services.

Even the purchase of small personal items such as an exercise bike can be underwritten to help develop demand. Equal payments with a low interest rate enable customers to get value in parallel with their use. Creating a benefit stream that matches the cost stream helps create demand for the product.

How Important Are Ecosystem Partners?

Why partner? Many companies with information-based products can now sell directly to customers and are questioning the need to use distribution channels. Cutting out partners in order to sell directly to the consumer, or "disintermediating" the distribution channel, has held a great deal of attention in business and some notable successes over the past few years. Dell, of course, has shown the potential for large companies to sell directly to the customer, through the Web and via the telephone.

Now that customers in general are more powerful and knowledgeable, doesn't it make sense to work directly with them to solve their problems? Doesn't it also make sense to provide the best possible price to customers by reducing the layers of distribution that must be paid out from the final customer price? The answer is, it depends.

In the technology industry, for example, the drive for growth without capital investment has been a major factor in using partners to go to market. Few can imagine the software industry today without extensive partnerships. Understanding and mastering partnerships is a core competency of software market leaders.

Telecommunications and networking companies also rely heavily on alliances and partner networks to create demand for their products. Their intricately woven business relationships make it possible for them to create demand for complex technical products.

Each of the top three software companies has some form of partner network. IBM, although better known for hardware, is the largest vendor of software products in the world. Big Blue has a business partner network that is used for distribution of products and customization of its multitude of offerings from the core IBM group as well as its Lotus and Tivoli units. At the same time, it has a global consulting practice that targets the largest companies in the world with specialized, and increasingly respected, non-partisan advice. SAP, the third-largest software company at one point, rose rapidly through the ranks by way of its alliance network of major consulting firms. The combination of its software and the re-engineering wave of the mid-'90s caused a major growth spurt for SAP. Microsoft, the second-largest software firm in the world, has amassed great capability in the area of partnering and alliances to create and solidify demand for products.

Partnerships as Strategic Alliances

Business scholars Yves L. Doz and Gary Hamel define three key purposes of a partnership or "strategic alliance"[1]:

- ◆ Co-option—a means of working with potential competitors and complementary goods and services that allows new business to develop. For example, Avnet and Arrow Electronics collaborated to purchase third-place distributor VEBA Electronics. Anti-trust prevented either of the top two players in that market from taking the third-largest company, but together they purchased the company, then split it by geographic region: Avnet taking South America and Asia-Pacific, and Arrow taking North America.
- ◆ Co-specialization—a means of creating synergies from separate resources, positions, skills, and knowledge. A partnership between Bank of America and enterprise software maker SAP, for example, was designed to create services and software for mid-size customers of Bank of America. SAP created the functionality, while Bank of America provided the distribution channel and the banking services skills.
- ◆ Learning and internalization—a means of learning and adopting new skills and insights from a business ally. The key to alliances for this purpose is to identify duration and outcome expectations in advance. A strategic partnership between Toyota and General Motors to create the NUMMI

(New United Motor Manufacturing, Inc.) production facility in 1984 was designed to help General Motors to learn more about Japanese manufacturing and production techniques. The outcome of this venture has been successful vehicle production, access for Toyota to the North American market, and learning by GM that has successfully been adopted in the Saturn manufacturing facilities.

The strategic alliance is the marriage or at least courtship of equals to create and develop new business opportunity. The critical concepts to take away are *synergy*, *complementarities*, and *co-specialization*.

Partnerships as Linked Business Models

The viability of a partnership strategy is based on all participants being able to support the business models of the partner organizations. Each business has a slightly different way of earning revenue and profit; if organizations that try to partner do not have any way of providing, funneling, or leveraging revenue to their partners, the partnership has no means of sustaining itself. Partnerships are fundamentally about increasing returns to partners.

When business models are complementary, the results for both partners include stability and growth. For years, electronics and semiconductor components distributor Arrow Electronics maintained a high-volume, low-margin business distributing assemblies and semiconductors for Intel, AMD, and other large manufacturers. From the manufacturers' perspective, there was little differentiation among distributors. From the customers' perspective, there was little to distinguish not only among distributors but also among manufacturers. Arrow Electronics and others in the sector began to add technical and engineering services that served to create specialized, even customized applications for the electronics parts it distributed. Under major threat from new online distributors and marketplaces that would deal with the commodity demand for undifferentiated products, Arrow was able to change its business model to derive new revenues from the demand for services and new loyalty from both customers and their suppliers. This also placed the company in a more effective position to influence the context of demand for the parts it distributed.

Partnerships as Biological Systems

Continuing our biological theme is the idea that partnerships act as biological agents for extending the customer ecosystem. Some of the key characteristics that make market partnerships resemble biological systems[2] include:

- **Autonomy**—The parts of the customer ecosystem function on their own, with their own economic incentives and their own decision-making capabilities, but within a system. Within electronics and semi-conductors ecosystem, Motorola makes decisions entirely separately from the decisions made by its key distributors, like Avnet and Arrow Electronics.

- **Metabolism**—Participants in the customer ecosystem require revenue and expend resources to create services and products, and their ability to function is regulated by the way in which their metabolism is structured. For example, the higher margins earned from specialized services by Arrow Electronics motivates it to provide more of those services. This is supported by its suppliers and by its customers.

- **Survival instinct**—Effective ecosystem partnerships provide enough benefit for each partner to ensure a willingness to prolong them. Relationships between electronics suppliers like Motorola and its distributors hit rocky ground when it appeared that new partners may be emerging online that would do the same functions as the distributors more efficiently and effectively. Distributors like Avnet then changed the way they did business to ensure that they would survive.

- **Evolution and adaptation**—Partnerships that can evolve with changing demand conditions are obviously more likely to last, but the ability to adapt depends on all the players being able to adapt. Kmart, long a highly valued supplier of low-cost goods, has not been able to change with market conditions and changing customer demands. It tried to adopt some of the methods of its arch-rival in the discount department store market, Wal-Mart, but has not been able to evolve. In contrast, Wal-Mart has been able to evolve and adapt to local markets, in order to continually grow with the customer needs, most recently extending its ecosystem into a supporting market—the used car market. In select locations, Wal-Mart will be leasing space to a national used car chain hoping to capitalize on the broad range of customers attracted to Wal-Mart sites.

From the biological metaphor perspective, we can see the value of interdependency among business partners is important only if it provides value to customers and to markets.

Building an Ecosystem of Demand:
The Windows NT Gambit

In 1998, Microsoft decided to get serious about the business market. Already dominating the desktop of businesses in North America, it had been developing its New Technology (NT) operating system as a network operating system (NOS) for several years but had yet to achieve the level of dominance that it knew was necessary to continue to grow in the business marketplace. Novell, its primary competitor in small business, was fading because its network operating system did not offer functionality as rich as the NT system offered. In the larger enterprise segment, a variety of suppliers (including IBM, Sun Microsystems, and Hewlett-Packard) offered a range of versions of the same basic operating system—the UNIX platform.

Few accomplished technologists and technology analysts really considered the NT operating system to be serious competition for the much more reliable, robust, and flexible UNIX operating systems. In addition, the combined might of three highly respected firms ought to be enough to hold back the upstart Microsoft. Most industry experts agreed that the desktop juggernaut was clearly was out of its league in the business market.

Yet, in about a year to 18 months, Microsoft was able to leverage an entire industry to support its expansion. The market was attacked on many fronts, and while Microsoft seemed to the press and the general public as arrogant, selfish monopolists, its partner network felt quite differently. What unfolded in the software industry was a network of partners with different roles, but each with greater ability to build its business through a partnership with Microsoft than without it.

The strength of the gambit was a result of the variety and breadth of partnership types, with as many as six categories operating at one time.

Demand Aggregators
◆ Microsoft Certified Solution Providers are considered part of the "channel." They are resellers of hardware and software that operate on the Microsoft NT platform. In order to be designated an MCSP, a business must have technical staff that is certified on Microsoft technology.

Syndicators
◆ Original equipment manufacturers are the hardware manufacturers that bundled NT software with higher-end network servers. Key beneficiaries were Dell and Compaq, which could offer lower-cost equipment to smaller firms competing with the likes of IBM and HP. Interestingly, IBM and HP did not want to miss out on the party either and offered both NT and Unix equipment to customers.

Integrators

◆ Microsoft Certified Professionals are the individuals that do the technical work for the NT network. Various levels of certification are available and, with that, improved earning and career opportunity.

◆ Microsoft Certified Solution Developers are software development companies (like Pivotal Corporation) that build applications to run on the NT platform. Recognition, marketing, and financial support are provided to companies that develop new functionality that brings new users, business or consumer, that will ultimately end in a platform win for Microsoft.

Educators

◆ Microsoft Certified Training Centers provide courses on Microsoft network technology. Marketing support and quality control for courses are provided to companies that work to educate technical workers on Microsoft's operating system.

This is only a partial listing of the complex web of programs that help to create demand for Microsoft products. In comparison with competitors, it appears that no other companies have brought forth such an interconnected approach with so many different moving parts.

While controversy rages about how Microsoft bundles the Internet Explorer software, by far Microsoft's biggest unsung victory has been in growing the market for business software, creating huge benefit for its entire partnership network.

Leveraging Ecosystem Partners

Finance

Broad networks of influential associates are critically important for success in financial markets. In the lending game, lawyers and accountants are indirect partners who can be a critical source of new business for high-end lenders.

For equity markets, companies like Yorkton Securities, a leading investment bank based in Toronto, Canada, can no longer afford to be loosely organized about their partner networks. For every financing opportunity that the managers consider, they systematically contact that company's board members and venture capital partners to develop relationships that will help the bank in both the short term and the longer term.

The systematic approach to covering each company enables Yorkton to be more effective and efficient in subsequent deals. "We find that the more deals we do using this approach, the more repetition of the players involved," notes Neil Smith, Director of Institutional Sales.

Insurance

In many insurance markets, in order to sell insurance, one must be a licensed broker. So for most companies there is really no getting around the established network, short of building your own network. Allstate Insurance, for example, works through a network of agents who are solely engaged with Allstate products. This network has taken many years and significant investment to build.

Choice, however, remains an important element of the buying decision for insurance customers. In health insurance, established networks may be the only route to market. Consumers expect to work with certain brands like Blue Cross/Blue Shield and will ask for those brands by name. This means that other companies targeting the same customers need to be working with those agents who carry that brand.

American Medical Security Group is a preferred provider organization (PPO) insurance carrier based in Green Bay, Wisconsin. To get to the consumer, AMS works with over 20,000 independent insurance agents, servicing 32 states in the U.S. In order to support this network, AMS has two primary regions, managed by regional vice presidents, with 70 sales managers distributed throughout the states covered.

"Trust is really a big issue for us, especially in terms of our relationship with our intermediaries, since their role (in the market) changes over time. In the short term, their role may be fairly strong, but in the long term, the relationship is bound to change," says Mark Seghers, Vice President of E-Business Development. "The way I see things, we need to hold on to the demand management and processes as long as possible. When it gets to the point that they're no longer serving our purposes well, then we need to change them."

Other companies have attempted a direct connection with the consumer through the Internet, by enabling customers to sign directly with them, but then assigning an agent to the renewal. The agents receive a lower commission on the renewals, but they are still involved in customer retention and maintaining the client relationship.

In addition to equipping sales managers with a customer management system to be better able to support independent agents, AMS is planning to implement a partner network system to provide its agents with information and support specifically for AMS products. Maintaining trust with its partners is a critical element in the design of this network.

Industrial Products

Traditional products like industrial equipment have usually used a distribution channel, due to the need to fit a product to a specific application. Industrial products are almost never purchased as single items, unless for replacement or repair; they are purchased as part of a solution or application. In order to do this, a range of partners is often required.

Holophane Lighting, a manufacturer of industrial lighting products for parking lots, stadiums, and factories, sold through traditional channels that mostly include specialist construction and engineering firms. When they added a new class of partners, the industrial architect, to their mix, they recognized that something had been missing. The contribution of expertise from the architects enabled them to create more compelling and creative applications for their mutual customers. Fundamentally, architect partners for Holophane combine aspects of the educator and the integrator demand development partners described earlier.

How to Implement Ecosystem Partnerships

Find the Standards That Matter

All ecosystems have some common currency—the DNA, if you will—of shared purpose that creates the mutual self-interest necessary to create a broader industry or market. Whether it is the networking standard of Bluetooth for wireless devices, the Windows operating system, or the standards of zoning and escrow in real estate, standards enable a broader concept of demand.

Many times the authors have heard one company or another declare itself the "de facto standard" of some narrowly defined industry. Marketing and strategy experts tell us that the best strategy is to be the only player in a sufficiently large market, which gives market power and the benefits of near-monopoly power. This is the motivation to be the "de facto standard" for a narrow segment. Most people interpret this as the *only* source of product or service of its kind. This is exactly the opposite of what we believe standards should be about. Without widespread collaboration by demand development partners, a standard does not exist.

Build, Change, Renew, Adapt Partnerships

Deal-driven collaboration is often necessary on specialized services, like public infrastructure construction projects. Creating a new highway or new stadium requires that companies be able to create relationships with new partners as new projects emerge. While many researchers term these relationships "strategic alliances," the ad-hoc relationship itself is not strategic; rather it is the ability of the firm to recreate new alliances for new purposes or projects that is the real strategic asset.

In addition, the kinds of partners that exist in reality may combine many of the characteristics required from a demand development partner. That is, partners may combine many different characteristics of the integrator, aggregator, syndicator, educator, and underwriter that are necessary for demand development.

Compete and Collaborate with Partners

In some markets, competitors may need to collaborate to build a market that is viable for both themselves and their competitors. This is a variation on the recombinant network discussed above. For some companies it is difficult to attune the culture to work with competitors. As with natural ecosystems, competition and collaboration both improve the viability of demand ecosystems.

Ensure That Revenue Matches Your Partner's Business Model

The motivation for a demand aggregator is very different from the motivation for an integrator. For example, enzyme manufacturer Novozymes partners with distributors that specialize in certain industrial markets. They act much like integrators because of their market knowledge and are compensated for their specialization in two ways: first, by relatively generous commissions on sales, and second, by adequate access to customers and technical support. Other distributors may not want or need the technical support and thus may receive incentives to turn product over more rapidly.

While these examples may sound like simple channel economics, far too many companies take a one-size-fits-all approach to their partner relationships. Few companies that are actually ecosystem leaders think strategically about the overall health of their supporting ecosystems. They need to adopt a more tailored approach to supporting indirect demand.

Notes

1. Yves L. Doz and Gary Hamel, *Alliance Advantage: The Art of Creating Value Through Partnering*, Harvard Business School Press, 1998.
2. Adapted from Melanie Mitchell, *Life and Evolution in Computers*, Santa Fe Institute Working Paper, No. 00-01-001, January 2001.

4

Step 3: Build Adaptive Strategies to Become Demand Driven

Ecosystems and Markets Are Adaptive

In nature, when a habitat is affected by stimulus of any kind, such as drought, new species introduction, or species extinction, there are usually several resulting impacts. One species may prosper and another may fail to survive, but the nature of the population within the habitat is constantly changing. At the edge of a deciduous forest in Mid-Atlantic States (New York, Pennsylvania, Ohio), for example, willows initially populate an open field of grasses and small poplars, then give way to maple and oak trees.

Customers within a market are not in any way static when a new product or other new stimulus is introduced into the market environment. Trial and adoption come slowly at first, and then sometimes the change is gradually accepted by the broad population. The old disappears and the new becomes standard. Customer demand for compact discs overtook records and cassette tapes, through a gradual process of technology adoption and diffusion.

Both Ecosystems and Markets Are Self-Organizing

Ecosystems will often have a keystone species (i.e., a species that directly or indirectly affects the abundance of other species. Removal of this species will cause upheaval for a period of time, but in time the structure of the community will find a way to re-regulate itself. Studies of rocky intertidal ecosystems (i.e., the marine life of the shores of saltwater bodies) show that, though the dominant species may change, the collective structure (in terms of number of species) will remain stable.

Customer, partner, and market relationships change and evolve over time. Customers may take stronger leadership roles in the relationship in certain markets and follower roles in others. Take, for example, the current two-horse race between Microsoft and the Java-based opposing computing standards from Sun Microsystems. Companies that participate in that market, left to their own means, build partnerships with the software market leader to fulfill some basic objectives: ensure that they can participate in each company's new market activities and hedge their bets in case one standard wins a greater share of the market. The partners themselves change—new companies emerging as start-ups, other companies changing sides, and still other companies failing and going out of business. The basic number of participants and the structure of two opposing sides balance and rebalance on their own.

Interactions Within Ecosystems and Within Markets Follow Common, Simple Rules

One rule that is emerging within ecosystems is an implied relationship between the number of different species and the population counts of each species. A broadly diverse ecosystem, such as in the tropical rainforests, will consist of many varieties of species, including some that are quite rare with very small populations counts. It is equally natural to have an ecosystem that has few species but large populations of each of those few species. When the current rules of the ecosystem change, the balance of ecosystem species diversity and species populations changes.

Ecosystems and Customer Relationships Can Experience Rapid and Accelerating Change

When an ecosystem's basic rules are changed, with the introduction of new participants or a sudden surge in the population of one species, the state of the system can change rapidly. In the Hawaiian Islands, from 1850 to 1920, several new species of birds were introduced without causing any decline in the number of native species. Then, after the introduction of other new species, the native species began to disappear at a very rapid rate. Scientists studying the issue suggest that there is a threshold level beneath which an ecosystem can absorb new participants; beyond that point, it will destabilize at a fairly rapid rate.[1]

In early 2000, the markets for telecommunications products like fiber optics had been growing at a rapid but linear pace for two to three years. All the major suppliers of these products—Cisco Systems, Nortel Networks, and others—were forecasting continued growth in demand for their products. Within months, a sudden turnaround on the part of customers occurred: they told the major players that now there was an excess capacity. The rapid turnaround in demand appeared to be a ripple effect from the crash of the dot-com companies that were the customers of the companies that fiber optics companies supplied.

Customer expectations are continually escalating as new capabilities for managing customer experience emerge. Add to that the continued increase in the number and form of intermediaries and other partners that the customer can access and you find a continually evolving and changing set of relationships. New sources of information in a marketplace can rapidly increase the pace of change just as new players can affect it.

Change in Ecosystems and Markets Appears Unpredictable

Cycles of fad and fashion continually confound market forecasters. Hush Puppies, for years the embodiment of old-fashioned, establishment footwear, found itself an unwitting participant in the haute couture runway shows of New York designers Anna Sui and Helmut Lang.[2] No advertising campaign created this demand; no integrated marketing campaign relaunched the brand. What can explain the sudden resurgence of Hush Puppies into the collective mindset of consumers? The re-emergence of Hush Puppies started with the adoption of vintage Hush Puppies by sophisticated, trend-setting New York club-goers. Leading designers like Sui and Lang, ever vigilant for street-savvy fashion, picked up the trend, which then found its way around the United States, transmitted by media and by cross-continental entertainment and fashion personalities. The linkages within this customer ecosystem were subtle but nonetheless powerful.

Because customers interact with competitors, your channel partners, and directly with you, managing relationships is hard, and gauging demand even harder. Additionally, customers have ever-increasing access to information and generally are more powerful in business relationships; the ability of businesses to predict their behavior is quite limited. In fact, the belief that consumer behavior can be predicted with simple projections and forecasts is very dangerous in today's markets. It is often more effective to anticipate ranges of behavior or ranges of preference than attempting to predict specific behavior.

Smaller Ecosystems Embed to Create Larger Ecosystems—Just as Smaller Market Relationships Embed to Create Larger Market Relationships

Even the tiniest grain of sand can contain an ecosystem, says renowned ecologist Edward O. Wilson in his recent book, *The Future of Life* (Knopf, 2002), and "a single coral head in Indonesia can harbor hundreds of species of crustaceans, polychaete worms and other invertebrates ..." plus an ecosystem of higher order swirling around them. From the microscopic to the macroscopic, patterns of life affect other patterns of life. So pervasive is the interconnection that some ecologists picture the entire surface of the earth, from the depths of the ocean to the tops of the rainforest canopies, as one connected entity.

Within the global telecommunications market, there are countless interdependent relationships between the end consumers of telephone airtime and the original suppliers of the switches and semi-conductors and fiber optics that make telephone communications possible. There are regional telephone connection suppliers in different countries and states within countries, long distance telephone suppliers that connect callers to fiber-optic backbones, parts suppliers and wholesalers, billing companies, and telephone outsourcers. Within a few blocks of anyone's home, there is likely to be a company that sells and installs telephone equipment, employing staff, paying a bookkeeper, and so on.

New Order Emerges out of Complete Disorganization

A set of rules or standards defines the arena in which an actor or agent will participate. Basic standards for business operations and the technical standards of the Internet combine to form the basic framework of the customer ecosystem. Without these rules, the system would be entirely unorganized, which would be defined as a chaotic system. But a complex system is not entirely chaotic, although it may appear to be at times.

Emergence of new properties within a complex system occurs as the result of the interaction of the agents with the structure and properties of the overall system. Interaction among organizations and individuals gives rise to new economic entities like we have discussed previously. Depending on the dynamics of the system, this may be predictable or unpredictable.

The Burning Need for Adaptive Strategy

The threat of new technologies and new orders arising from the existing ecosystems, along with the threat of control from the activist customer, implies the burning need for companies to take control of their own destiny. How do companies become more effective in dealing with their customer ecosystem?

By deploying adaptive strategies based on the need to both create new demand and service existing demand for customers that have varying degrees of potential control, companies can hedge their bets, not relying on the outcome of specific strategies, but being poised to capitalize on a range of outcomes.

Consider the wireless telephone customer ecosystem in North America, circa 2002. Two key players are competing on two very different messages to the marketplace. Verizon, in one corner, is using the very simple message "Can you hear me now?" to address the very simple need customers have for reliable wireless coverage on the existing wireless network. Sprint, in the other corner, is preparing to launch a data-driven third-generation (3G) wireless network, staking a large part of its customer ecosystem's development on the potential emergence of new demand for new wireless services.

Both are very risky positions. New technology could render the Verizon issue irrelevant and there is no telling if third-generation wireless technology will hold value for Sprint customers. Adaptive strategies enable companies to address the needs of today, while preparing for the future (see Figure 4-1).

A Portfolio of Adaptive Strategies

In order to capitalize on what is an inherently unpredictable market environment, many companies are turning to an approach that hedges their bets on their offerings. Companies must both create change in markets and be able to respond and adapt to change in their markets. In a complex adaptive system, waves of change can occur from many directions, originating from many different actors.

The creation of a portfolio of strategies is akin to having a portfolio of products or assets. The concept of a portfolio approach is to ride with a core strategy and core context, until the next big thing arises and it becomes obvious that it will make dramatic change on the industry.

Around 1998, many industry watchers felt that Microsoft had been late to the Internet party. In retrospect, it may have been another example of Microsoft hedging its bets, with a portfolio of strategies. While it became obvious to the company that it needed to put more effort into the Internet, it did not necessarily want to be just an Internet company. Microsoft continued its development and marketing efforts to build its hold on business networking and database infrastructure. Today, the NT software segment and its business network continue to grow and build, despite a downturn in the Internet sector.

Out of control:
- Low profitability, attractiveness
- Uncertain market viability
- Barriers to exit keep players in the game

Companies need more to control the rate of change in the market, in order to keep it viable. Demand-creation strategies can preempt markets being changed without participation of market incumbents.	Companies need more adaptability and control over customers and markets. Demand-creation strategies are required to counteract forces of changing demand and customer control.

High

Low

Influence of Indirect Demand

Complex, Adaptive Customer Ecosystem

Passive   Collaborator   Activist

Customer Activism

Assumes business as usual:
- high threat of disruptive technology changing nature of demand

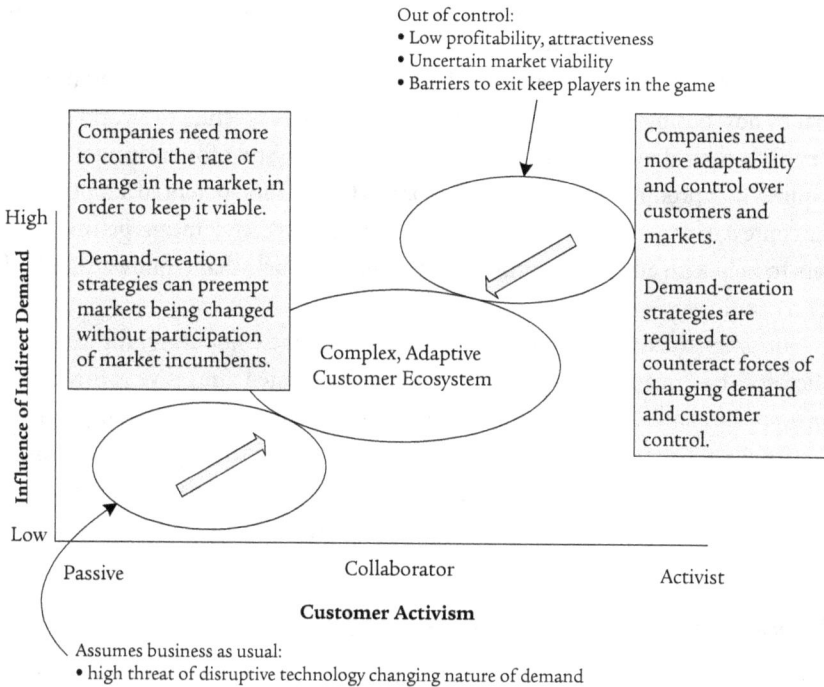

Figure 4-1. The driving forces of adaptive strategies

Shaping the Nature of Overall Ecosystem Demand

Creating and shaping demand for products is the hallmark of many consumer-oriented companies. It is also the strategy for innovative technology companies like Boeing and Sony. Finding and driving disruptive technologies has part of the collective culture of Silicon Valley for the past decade or more. Indeed, Gary Hamel, highly respected Harvard Business School researcher, penned an article advocating that companies should be "Bringing Silicon Valley Inside"[3] by finding ways to create a climate that produces radical technology innovation.

While there is a general fascination in today's culture for technology innovation, it takes much more to ensure that real business demand results from this innovation.

Strategies for creating demand manifest themselves both inside and outside the firm. Inside the organization, the creation of new technologies must be driven by encouraging experimentation and through focused research and development. Some companies go a step further and set objectives for the creation of new products, not leaving to chance the potential for creating new demand. General

Electric, for example, mandates that 25% of revenues must come from products introduced in the past five years.

Demand shaping requires more than product development. One would think that by now businesses would not fall into the trap of "expecting the world to beat a path to their door." Influencing the customer ecosystem for creating demand requires that products be pushed to customers for trial and potential adoption (in the context of actual purchase, not just use). More than ever, it means getting partners to help with adoption, particularly the new products that require a standard for technology.

In order to create the market for pervasive home computing, for example, Microsoft has created standards for software and hosted a massive gathering of software and hardware technology partners, the Windows Hardware Engineering Conference (WinHEC), to share information and develop strategy. The creation of broad-based demand for home network software, the company recognizes, is dependent not only on the adoption of one product, but also on the adoption of standards and a host of other products.

Responding to Direct Customer Demand

Companies respond to customer needs through a variety of strategies. Common approaches are to enable customers to customize products using more sophisticated software technology. Demand-responding strategies are characterized by ensuring that customers can assemble products or services to meet the needs of the situation.

Providing "over-the-top" excellence in service is not the only form of demand-responding strategies. Companies like Southwest Airlines have demonstrated that a high price isn't necessary to get great service. While serving the core demand for airline travel, the company has provided several innovations around the experience and delivery of that service. This does not mean that Southwest has not made strategic choices. Its choices have been around the activities that it undertakes to deliver the core offering.

First of all, it positioned on the obvious demand for lower-cost air travel and, in order to deliver the low-cost travel, it discovered that there were several activities that its competitors considered essential that it did not: assigned seats, in-flight meals, the hub-and-spoke routing system. Second, it also focused on customer service. Most important, it focused on understanding and adapting to the critical core factors that drive customer satisfaction, like on-time departure and arrival, not in-flight movies or other frills. The stripped-down experience has become part of the culture: packets of peanuts might be tossed at you by a flight attendant, in sharp contrast to the business-class experience of a three-course meal served on with china and silver.

Incremental innovation in customer service also occurred in its modes of contact: online flight browsing was introduced in 1996 and online flight booking capability was provided in 1998.

Creating Adaptive Ecosystem Strategies

The broader concept of customer ecosystem integration may incorporate technical integration of network or data protocols, but, most important, it looks at the concept of organizational integration with the source of direct and indirect customer demand. The key here is to focus the extended capabilities on the right set of demand management objectives.

How organizations approach extending capabilities is based on some choices, including strategic choice and customer relationship requirements. We have identified five basic approaches extending capabilities. In order to implement these approaches, companies must deploy technology-enabled activities to partners and customers as well as institutional competencies through like culture, organizational structure, and processes.

Prior to the advent of the network and Internet technologies, most companies really had only the capability to focus on one-way communications, in the promotion mode, the reaction mode, or the exchange mode (see Figure 4-2).

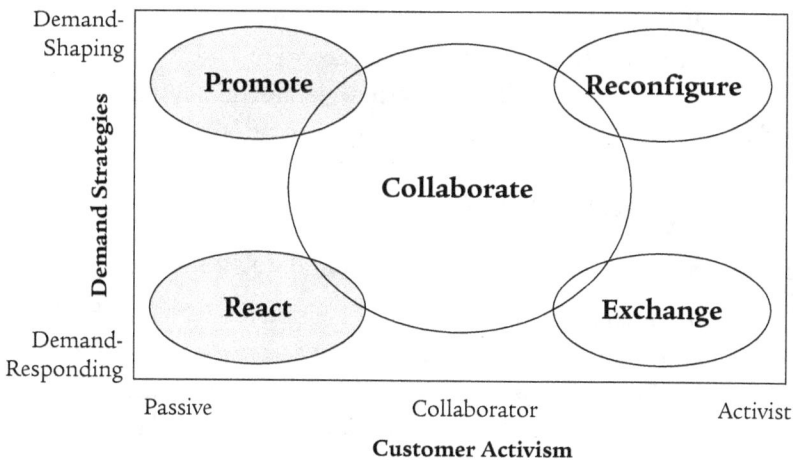

Figure 4-2. Framework for adaptive ecosystem strategies

Adaptive Strategies 1: Promote to Create Demand

Probably the most common set of strategies, promotion is appropriate when the primary customer orientation is mostly passive and the key concern is to shape demand. Traditional marketing strategies rely heavily on the one-way flow of information from supplier to customers to shape demand, that is, to create new demand for a product—communications that go directly to a customer.

Adaptive Strategies 2: React Effectively to Existing Demand

Typically, reaction strategies are appropriate in a commodity-like market. The key focus of these strategies is to enable transactions and interactions to be as low cost as possible. Little can be gained by overinvesting in improving the level of connection through technology or other communications methods, because the customer has little interest in more connection or in co-development.

Adaptive Strategies 3: Exchange Information to Respond to Active Customers

Exchange strategies in a customer ecosystem involve creating capabilities and activities that enable the exchange of information. The intent of exchange strategies is to respond effectively to customers that drive the business relationship.

Just-in-time exchanges in the manufacturing sector are good examples of exchange integration. The information that is transferred between the organization and the ultimate customer (the primary automotive manufacturer, for example) is highly task- or process-oriented.

Innovation strategies for product development or service development may be valuable but also may simply add cost to the service provided.

Customer relationship management strategies are critically important, ensuring that service responsiveness is a primary element of strategy. Information exchange will help to reduce sources of friction, so that the supplier is better able to respond to the needs of the customer.

Adaptive Strategies 4: Reconfigure Demand Relationships

When a company is caught in the position of a customer orientation that is dominant, that is, the customer is the value leader, the company will need to find ways to reconfigure the customer ecosystem to enable its strategies for demand creation to work. Old relationships and old modes of integration are unlikely to work.

Adaptive Strategies 5: Collaborate Where Possible

Most popular for companies attempting to engage more actively with their customers is the collaboration mode of adaptive strategy integration. Customers are willing to share control over the relationship and will respond to a combination of demand-creation and demand-response strategies.

Software-based collaborative applications for customer relationship management are very popular right now. Some of the popular concepts include online communities that enable customers to identify sources of value and issues of interest to them and product configuration tools. Other collaborative tools that are institutionally based are joint product development teams, used in many consumer products companies. In a later chapter, we will discuss the collaborative approach used by Proctor & Gamble and its ingredient supplier, Novozymes, to improve core products like Tide.

Notes

1. From Richard Sole and Brian Goodwin, *Signs of Life: How Complexity Pervades Biology* (New York: Basic Books 2002).
2. As explained by Malcolm Gladwell in his book, *The Tipping Point: How Little Things Can Make a Big Difference* (Boston: Little Brown & Company, 2000).
3. Gary Hamel, "Bringing Silicon Valley Inside," *Harvard Business Review*, September-October 1999.

5

Step 4: Use Information Technology to Support Your Ecosystem

T he bridge between the customer ecosystem and the business is information and communications technology. The origins of technology to manage a customer ecosystem are in customer relationship management (CRM) systems. This chapter is designed to provide a summary of the key components of CRM. The following chapter will provide perspective on how to utilize these components most effectively in a customer ecosystem.

There are really three main objectives of customer relationship management: increase revenue, decrease costs, and increase customer loyalty.

Enriching the Customer Experience Through Value-Added Information

Providing enhanced information to the empowered customer is one way that companies attempt to create more loyalty. Primarily using Internet technology, companies will enable the active customer with more information.

As a society, we are both inundated by information and at the same time starved for relevant information. Building a relationship with customers through relevant information is particularly effective in building trust and understanding.

Value-added information takes several forms:

◆ **Product information**, such as specifications, performance, and other detailed information not immediately communicated in a sound bite through outbound marketing information or a sales rep. Many consider this a basic, expected element of building relationship through value-added information.

◆ **Relationship information**, such as shipping status, gives a fact-based perspective on what is happening once a purchase is made. Knowing the location of the package that you shipped through an online tracking utility doesn't change its status, but it does inform the customer and manage expectations. Whether you get this information online or through a call center, it gives customers an increased understanding of the relationship status, which hopefully builds more trust into that relationship.

◆ **Decision support information.** Suppliers build relationship by answering questions like "How much will this car cost on a per-month basis?" and "What other products will I need if I purchase this router?" Providing information that helps to answer implications of purchase or relationship is intended to help give customers the feeling that the supplier is willing to help them sort out what it really means to them on a personal basis or for their specific situation. Sometimes, this kind of value-added information helps to dissuade a customer that is not a good fit for the product that you offer. And this is a good thing, because it is so much easier for the influential customer to spread information, as we discussed in the last chapter, and potentially disastrous if it is negative.

Integrating the Customer Experience Across Touchpoints

Touchpoints are channels or communications media, like direct sales contact, telesales and telemarketing, Web site, and customer service contact centers. And as consumers, we have all experienced a different kind of treatment through one touchpoint versus another. Calling a consumer help line may give rapid service, while waiting in a department store for an employee may seem to take hours and hours.

The need to undertake an integration project is the result of functional suboptimization in the parts of the organization that touch customers. That is, most companies start with a customer database for sales management, a customer database for direct marketing, and another few perhaps that deal with customer service problems. An integrated, single view of the customer is a critical requirement in a demand ecosystem—effective customer experience depends on the richness

Application: Cambridge Energy Research Associates

With a global business that runs across a number of continents and time zones, Cambridge Energy Research Associates (CERA) knew that its future depended on using Internet technology to stay in close touch with its clients. CERA, a 15-year-old, leading international independent energy research and advisory firm, serves more than 400 clients around the world. One of the most pressing issues for CERA was that it had no single, consistent, and fully rounded view of its customers. Understanding the broad set of customer needs through better customer information has enabled CERA to create new products that provide more value to customers.

At the heart of CERA's system are the innovative links it has built among various platform "connection points" with customers—including its password-protected, subscriber-based Web site, its internal intranet, its electronic mail system, and its call center.

"We consider ourselves a strategic knowledge company on one level, and on another we're a publisher," says a company executive. "One thing that quickly became clear to us was the compelling economics of delivering knowledge to our clients via the Web. It was obvious that we were eventually going to need to move our business to a Web-based model.

"We've taken what some have called pioneering steps in integrating our Web-based knowledge services with our customer information and customer relationship management system ... for managing the Web 'permissioning' of our clients (so that only users with paid subscriptions can access the premium portions of the Web site). [The system] also logs critical information about our clients' access and use of CERA's knowledge on the Web."

This also means improved customer service. "Customers can now enjoy 7x24 access to the knowledge services to which they are entitled," CERA reports. "As we learn more about how much customers use the site—since all of that is being sent back directly to our customer relationship system—it then becomes available to the entire CERA organization. It's becoming a means of better informing CERA about who is using what and who is interested in what, and in so doing, it's becoming a very powerful tool for channeling feedback and helping us craft better products and services to meet clients' needs."

and accessibility of customer information throughout the network of demand. Starting with a simple customer record management system, organizations need to be able to ensure access to customer information across virtually all organizational areas. Many notable companies have undertaken massive efforts to integrate these databases to ensure that an issue or opportunity in one part of the business is not overlooked in another part of the business.

Many companies install CRM technology to provide customers with the right to choose how they will be serviced—by telephone, by Internet, in person, or by e-mail. This ensures that, regardless of channel, customers will get accurate personal treatment.

Farm Credit Services of America: Customer Care Champions

In the financial services industry, organizing business around product and service offerings was once the norm. Employees had highly specialized areas of expertise, a top priority considered in the best interest of the customer. What's changed? Now it's deep customer relationships, not just product and service knowledge, that companies count among their most valued assets and that is the key to competitive advantage. Today they encourage team selling, with many product and service specialists working together to meet customer needs.

Farm Credit Services of America, based in Omaha, Nebraska, is dedicated to serving the agricultural credit and financial needs of farmers and ranchers. FCSAmerica's 46,000 customers live and work the thousands of rural farms and ranches in Iowa, Nebraska, South Dakota, and Wyoming. As a result, many of its financial officers are on the road long hours, traveling the dusty and remote roads that lead to their clients' farms.

Three years ago, FCSAmerica began reorganizing employees to deliver more specialized services and product knowledge in response to customer needs. However, they didn't have the internal systems in place to support the financial officers—all leasing, accounting, loan, and insurance data were isolated in disparate systems. Explained Jim Greufe, Director of CRM Implementation: "Even though we wanted an integrated customer view, we didn't have the customer relationship management system to support these new roles. We've worked hard to integrate all our disparate systems and to support our field employees with the means to understand customer needs with a unified customer view regardless of the interaction channel—whether face to face, over the phone, or via e-mail."

Migrating Customers to Lower-Cost or Self-Service Channels

The advantages of using automation to lower business costs are obvious. For banks, as an example, it costs $1.15 for live service through a teller, $0.36 for an automated teller, and $0.20 for online transactions. Not surprisingly, most companies are seeking ways to service customers increasingly through technological means. Under the guise of CRM, companies present the technology tools as more accessible and more effective for the customers, regardless of their initial resistance.

Evaluating cost to service requires that companies can estimate or specify the frequency of customer problems, repairs, or inquiries. As discussed above, tracking the interactions with customers can ensure that their needs are being met and that they have no problem or cause that leads to dissatisfaction. Just because a client buys a lot from you doesn't mean it is profitable.

Application: Chancery Software

Chancery Software, a leading software developer in the K-12 education market, has been learning lessons from its customers about ways to serve them better.

The extension of technical support to the Internet is important to Chancery because of its large customer base. Some 350,000 educators and administrators throughout North America use Chancery's student information systems to manage information on over five million students. Providing timely, effective, and efficient support to all these users has represented a major challenge—and an opportunity for Chancery. Chancery realized that the Internet could be a valuable medium in helping to meet this challenge. A self-service support Web site could improve the service offered to Chancery's customers. In addition, given that Chancery had a high transaction cost each time a customer needed to interact with a live customer support representative, there was significant financial incentive to move customers to self-service support as well. Chancery's technical support Web site represented the "frontline" of the company's connection to its customers—where a good experience wins long-term customer satisfaction while a poor one can lead to a lost account.

For Devon Boorman, Support Technology Manager at Chancery Software, the greatest challenge has been to create a solution that will provide effective support for a wide range of customers. "In the beginning, we posted a lot of static pages with questions and answers to technical problems on our

---

Web site," he recalls. "We had 1,000 of these pages, but our support reps and customers found it difficult to search for the information they needed."

Boorman knew that, in order for customers to want to use Web-based services, Chancery would have to provide at least as good an experience to users as through telephone support. So Chancery used a Web-based solution to extend its customer support system out to the Web. He says this has allowed users who visit the site to quickly and simply build their own, custom-created support pages containing the help information they really need. It has also cut down the number of static pages within Chancery's support site from 1000 to a mere 10.

Personalizing the Customer Experience

The one-to-one marketing concept of combining personalized information with mass customization, popularized by Martha Rogers and Don Peppers, has taken the industry by storm.

What does personalization do? In many ways, it enables a brand or product to reflect the personal attitudes or preferences of a customer. Personalization can range from the simply cosmetic—meaning that a Web site or letter is personalized with an individual's name—to the fully customized—meaning that both the interface and the attributes of a product are changed for an individual.

True personalization is no simple task, although it definitely should seem simple to the customer. It can require a massive amount of data management capacity and a robust process for defining the rules for responding to the personal or unique requirements.

Holophane: Efficiency and Effectiveness Through CRM

After more than 100 years in business, Newark, Ohio-based Holophane Corporation knows that making customers happy is vital to the success of its business. Holophane has built a $200 million annual revenue base by being a leading international manufacturer and marketer of premium-quality, highly engineered lighting fixtures and systems for a wide range of industrial, commercial, and outdoor applications.

Much of its success is directly attributable to the work of Holophane's direct sales team, which is known within the industry for its work in providing customized lighting design and product assistance in creating lighting solutions based on unique customer needs.

Holophane realized that if the company was to grow an average of 10% annually, it was going to have to make some significant changes in the way it operated. According to Douglas J. Stang, the Manager of Holophane's Information Services Department, the company mapped out its current and ideal sales and order processing steps and concluded that a flexible CRM technology would significantly improve the way it operated. Although Holophane's strength has always been in its ability to "mass customize" its products, complexity and time-consuming bottlenecks in the order entry cycle contributed to manufacturing errors, reschedules, expedites, and excessive handling of information and paperwork. This resulted in more than one-third of orders being sent back for clarification and 52% of ordering requiring changes after order entry. Making those changes was expensive and time-consuming—as well as being frustrating for Holophane's customers. The new CRM system solved these problems.

Differentiating Treatment by Customer Value

Selecting the right customers is critical not only to customer loyalty, but also to short-term business profitability. Many companies find that a small proportion of their customers contribute a great proportion of their revenue and profits. The well-known Pareto principle, also commonly known as the 80-20 rule, applies to almost every company's customer base.

Customer value analysis is a complicated thing sometimes. In financial services, a typical middle-aged working parent will have a mortgage, some investments, savings and checking accounts, and a range of insurance products and other savings tools. Profitable customers, so the logic goes, buy more products from you and cost less to market to. Analytical tools help companies to move from the idealized concepts of one-to-one marketing to the real-world implementation. Specifically, identifying the right customers requires analysis that will rank customers on number of transactions, total value of their transactions, and/or customer tenure (also known as loyalty).

The Functional Building Blocks

The state of the art in CRM provides a basis for customer capabilities—this is *the minimum standard for entrepreneurial enterprises*. To compete for customers today, large and small businesses require some of the functionality that we will describe.

Each element of the technology has related elements of business process. We will describe later how this evolves into business capability.

Marketing Functions

The critical building blocks of CRM from a marketing perspective include e-mail-enabled, highly targeted, highly personalized, and permission-based.

One caveat, however: especially for marketing purposes, CRM requires accuracy of customer records. It is estimated that about 20%-35% of the total records within a marketing database are inaccurate at any given time. Customer information cannot just correct itself; procedures and processes for checking records, passively when customers make contact or actively through outbound activities, ensure the validity and value of customer data.

E-mail-enabled. Integration with e-mail for marketing purposes is an obvious requirement for businesses today. That e-mail surpassed the telephone in 1999 as the preferred means of communications for business should not surprise anyone. But for marketing purposes, e-mail-enabled customer relationship management systems mean much more. To be effective, they must enable quality graphics and flexible group distribution as well as the fluid connection with marketing campaign information.

Highly targeted. Centralized databases are central to the value proposition of CRM technology pitches. Yet the value of the central information is lost without the ability to extract information to finely segment the customers in that database. In order to extract value, companies must easily create highly targeted customer offerings.

In order to do this, marketing users must be able to get at customer data and create profiles without requiring an advanced education in database management. Creating complex queries should be as easy as creating the targeted message that you intend to send forward.

Highly personalized. Once potential customers are attracted or involved with a supplier, highly personalized CRM functionality provides the ability to respond in a highly relevant, personal way.

Technologies for managing personalization typically resemble the online profile systems of the My Yahoo! variety, which enable customers and prospects with some form of password-protected personal Web page. But highly personalized also means that, regardless of channel, customers will be treated as though you know them.

Permission-based. Permission marketing is a very popular communications concept, originated by Seth Godin, to describe a process that "turns strangers into friends and friends into customers." The concept of permission-based marketing has implications for CRM from two important levels: 1) strict adherents to permission marketing concepts[1] need to utilize a fairly sophisticated ability to distinguish among customers with varying levels of interest in an offer; 2) all marketers need to be able to manage permission to some degree to gain any level of trust with potential customers.

In order to manage permission, companies have several options, ranging from the passive management to the active management, all of which depend heavily on linkages to permission information among the various customer touchpoints.

Example: While most companies' permission approaches are Web- or e-mail-based, call centers remain an important part of customer service operations. If a leading retailer like Lands' End were unable to link Web permission strategies with call center strategies, customers would not only be surprised, but many would be annoyed.

Closed loop. One of the major changes in marketing that has arisen over the last few years is the expectation that marketing is accountable for proving the value of the investment in communications and promotions programs. Without a closed loop system that tracks outbound marketing activities right through to completion of the sale and that also ensures the ability to learn and improve from the results, marketing professionals cannot be held accountable for the value of their efforts. CEOs and investors no longer tolerate a "black box" approach to the development of new business.

Shared customer databases that track communications throughout the lead-to-customer loop are necessary tools to ensure that marketers can learn more about customers and improve their efforts.

Sales Functions

Frontline contact with customers for most businesses is through a mobile, professional sales force. The real roots of demand management and the customer ecosystem concept begin with the early attempts at customer databases, sales force automation, contact management, and the like.

This particular function of CRM began as a mostly inwardly focused objective. This is the domain where most organizations have been disappointed with their forays into customer relationship management. Frequently seen by capable, and less capable, salespeople as a "Big Brother" technology—suitable only for oversight and extending control—sales force automation has achieved spectacular results for some organizations and has been a colossal nuisance for others.

When you get it right, it is to focus on how efficiency of the sales process contributes to satisfaction for both customer and employee. It also can be the basis of extended capabilities—helping customers to create value for themselves through communications and network technology.

Sales process methodology. The sales process can be made much more effective and rigorous through automation. This, of course, was one of the original reasons for adopting front office technology (a.k.a. sales force automation, contact management) in organizations.

From a business advantage viewpoint, managing the sales process through CRM can benefit customers if, in fact, customers value a more consultative approach. Managing the steps and stages that enable a comprehensive solution is often better for the customer, to ensure quality, and for the supplier, to ensure greater success.

What this really means is that software can guide a sales team through a unique but common set of steps for:

♦ Identifying explicit and implicit customer needs, whether they are technical, social, or ego-related
♦ Mapping and understanding buyer influence
♦ Identifying issues and pre-empting buyer objections, not just reacting to them

Comprehensive lead sourcing and management. It's an ongoing saga in business today: sales managers question the relationship between marketing campaign effectiveness and actual closed sales. In worst-case scenarios, sales points the finger at poor quality leads and marketing points the finger back at sales, citing a lack of follow-up. The solution, of course, begins with an integrated database approach and continually loops around with constant re-examination of both issues: which lead sources provide the best close rate and what is the follow-up on leads generated by the marketing group.

One company that implemented a CRM system found a way to ensure that this conflict occurred, by having marketing use a separate lead management system to manage lead generation and its sales team manage the sales process in individual contact management systems. The company successfully set up several islands of information that were supplemented by a weekly spreadsheet of new leads for the entire company, sent to each of the regional sales representatives. The very successful lead generation team could produce at least a hundred new leads each week that 35 regional sales reps were to pick from the spreadsheet. Out of the hundreds of leads each month, fewer than a handful would get a follow-up call and, of course, no one could evaluate the true quality of the leads being generated.

Rich, multi-source information/intelligence. The motto for this building block is the old Boy Scout motto—"Be Prepared." Equipping a sales team with information about customers, products, and competitors is invaluable to supplement the skill and savvy of today's professional sales team. Especially when coupled with sales methodology, a salesperson with the information at his or her fingertips about a prospect's financial status or recent press releases (good or bad) can make a much more effective use of time.

Web services can deliver this information automatically to the desktop of a sales representative. And as long as the salesperson utilizes the information, he or she arrives at a prospect's business prepared to be more relevant and more effective than the competition.

Proposal generation. Persuasion, influence, and effectiveness are all enhanced by proposal generation technology. Enabling flexible proposal generation technology means that a salesperson can create an effective presentation of a company's offering without struggling through the sometimes grueling process of writing a proposal from scratch.

From a technical perspective, proposal generation depends on a software utility to guide a salesperson through a content selection and structuring process and then to flag text from a database to be merged into a document that is personalized and customized for specific customer requirements.

Automated forecasting. Sales forecasting is one of the most reviled yet critically required administrative exercises in the sales function of most organizations. Inaccurate, untimely sales forecasts from the field sales force can drive the chief financial officer into fits of rage and despair. As witnessed throughout the turn of the new millennium and continuing at the time of this writing, the quarterly sales forecast for major corporations can send share prices into either a wild plummet or a modest upward trend.

Automating the forecasting process can save sales managers significant effort compared with the traditional process of combining spreadsheets or handwritten forms faxed into the head office. When combined with standard rules for valuing the potential of individual sales deals, automated forecasting functionality can even support some of the process of reducing the forecast probabilities provided by eternally optimistic, special breed of people on the frontlines of the sales function.

What is required to provide automated forecasting is simple: a shared opportunity database, mobile synchronization or pervasive Web access to a central system, and the guidance of a senior sales professional to ensure relevance and timeliness of the forecast data.

Interactive Selling

Interactive selling capabilities for products and services online are increasingly easy and robust. Direct sellers like Dell and Cisco pioneered the online configuration and guided selling of computers and other complicated technology products. Other companies, like auto manufacturers, today give customers the opportunity to tailor their products.

Online customer experience is often linked closely with the extended functionality of the online applications for customer transactions. To what extent do customers enjoy or find useful the transaction functionality that they are provided? The linkage of online functionality for customers with the rest of the business has evolved from a strategic question (Do we have a separate Web store business or do we integrate it?) to a strategic necessity (We must be able to offer the same goods and service online as in the rest of our business!).

Required building blocks of interactive selling include a comprehensive, personalized dictionary, configuration, personalized pricing, needs analysis, and intuitive authoring.

Comprehensive, personalized dictionary. "A place for your stuff." That's what comedian and social commentator George Carlin said. "We all need a place for our stuff." Even online, we need a place for the information that is relevant and personal and meaningful to each of us, especially in relation to the products and services that we want to buy. When you go to VW.com, you have a place for your stuff: there you can save the make and model of car that you are interested in along with any financing information. At Lands' End you can save a "My Virtual Model™" replica of yourself (surprisingly accurate!) along with the clothes that you want to wear.

For customers, a comprehensive, personalized dictionary provides the basis of relationship and trust that is necessary for loyalty and for repeat purchase.

For suppliers, this means that you need to provide the ability to set aside not only a shopping cart, but a wish list or some semblance of preferences for easy access by your customers at some later occasion.

Configuration. Unique requirements require unique solutions. As a society, we are fortunate that our ability to address unique requirements with technology has advanced so far. Among the tools at our disposal, the ability to interactively configure a product to our personal requirements is both commonplace and productive. As mentioned above, companies selling products like computers and network hardware have pioneered the means to identify the specific elements of a product that a customer wants.

To do this, configuration of products online must be linked to operational processes in a robust manner. This means that if a certain combination of product characteristics is not feasible in a real, operational sense, there should not be any way to make this combination in the virtual configuration process.

Personalized pricing. "Personalized pricing" is a much better term than "price discrimination." (Let's not put price discrimination on the same plane as race or sex discrimination, after all.) Classical microeconomic theory tells us that consumer needs are maximized when individual needs are maximized at the price consumers are willing to pay. For each of us this is likely some different function. Based on whatever individual combination of product or service, we each respond differently to a given price.

Configuration, personalized pricing, accounting for product choices, and negotiated terms or frequent purchaser status make up the key capabilities for personalization.

Needs analysis. What if you don't know what product you really want to buy or only vaguely know the general parameters of your requirements? Online selling technology today can help the novice cyclist to narrow down rapidly his or her set of choices, based on price and intended use, from 200 different models of bicycles to four or five mountain bikes in the $300-$500 range that work well for mild trail riding on a weekly basis.

Intuitive authoring. One of the authors regularly teaches e-commerce marketing to MBA students. Toward the end of the semester, this question is posed: "How much should marketers know about technology?" In most classes, the debate is lively, given the mix of engineering, finance, and marketing students that the course seems to attract. The question resonates generally in marketing circles, but more often than not gets the response that marketers really don't need to know about technology; they merely need to apply it. This is most certainly also the case for interactive selling. Intuitive authoring of online selling processes and online configuration functionality must be such that even a marketer can operate the controls. It is the marketer's job to envision the implications of the configuration or guided selling process on the customer experience. But a marketer does not need to truly understand the technology; the software system should be as intuitive as possible.

What does it take to provide this functionality? This is actually sophisticated technology. Intuitive authoring requires an easy-to-use, front-end interface that drives the creation of complex code in a back-end system by linking to a database of commands and code combinations. This back-end system, in turn, generates the desired online choices for potential customers.

Customer Service Functions

Embraced as the key to success for managing customer relationships by companies like Xerox and IBM, customer satisfaction today is a key element of building a customer ecosystem. Satisfaction, it is claimed, is a necessary condition for loyalty. It is certainly a necessary condition for an effective customer experience. Without customer satisfaction, the experience may not develop over time.

Automated call handling. Customers with problems have very little patience—as consumers we all agree. The faster a problem is acknowledged and dealt with, the greater the potential to salvage any shred of relationship with that customer. When consumers take the time to call, it is possible to disarm the irate customer with a pleasant "Hello, Mr. Manning, how are you enjoying that last book you purchased?" Even more effective is the automatic routing of a call to the senior technician who is currently looking into the causes of your hardware failure for the half-million-dollar plastic injection molding equipment that is costing your company losses by the hour.

In both of these scenarios, customer records must "pop" when calls are routed to service staff. The ability to do this is dependent on the linkage of digital telephone systems and customer relationship management systems.

Comprehensive knowledge management. If only it were possible to staff your customer service center with the most experienced service people at the cost that enables you to stay competitive in the marketplace! The reality of customer service is that it is not a long-term job for most employees, often resulting in inexperienced staff answering difficult questions. Providing knowledge management tools to the customer service staff supports the less experienced service rep and helps customers to get resolution more quickly.

What's required here is that resolution information is recorded and systematized and publicized for use by all customer service staff. Automated information processing, open data access, and even "fuzzy logic" searches enable knowledge to be shared more readily.

Empowered/enabled agents. As consumers, the very thought of having to call a customer service line may get our blood boiling. It is particularly vexing when we have invested minutes or hours of our time on hold, waiting for an agent, who then attempts to tell us to hold while he or she gets the supervisor.

The empowered agent is the answer, but how can CRM technology help with this? Standard procedures, full access to customer history and customer account information, and customer value assessment information provide the context for making judgment calls. The ability to schedule service calls or to adjust the financial status of accounts means that action can happen on the spot.

From a technology point of view, integration with billing and service scheduling is paramount to enabling agents to diffuse any customer issue by creating activities for other customer service agents or other key individuals that support customers. Standard procedures and activity management are created through workflow tools.

Rigorous incident management. Customer service business process automation can be the single most important objective of many CRM applications. For those customers who seek to improve satisfaction and loyalty by managing the process of customer service, leading vendors have built highly effective and highly specialized systems to manage the process by which a company ensures that it solves customer problems and responds to customer inquiries rapidly and effectively.

The basic requirement for incident management is to automate service-level standards in terms of how quickly customers with problems receive responses and have their problems resolved. In order to ensure that each and very problem is resolved, it is also a basic requirement that there is a system for tracking customer problems. Thus, the trouble ticket, problem escalation, product or service "knowledge base" functionality has become part of the everyday verbiage of customer service staff. Given that most customer service organizations had little or no process automation and solving problems as rapidly as possible is now *de rigueur,* customer service process automation has been among the more successful applications of CRM technology.

Multiple-channel support/integration. The ability to handle customer inquiries via phone, fax, e-mail, or live online "chat" enables customer service organizations to ensure that customers are treated effectively regardless of preferred communications channel.

Universal queue management. Too often, customer service inquiries fall through the cracks if a company is set up to handle only the occasional e-mail or fax inquiry. Most CRM systems are set up to handle phone interactions effectively, but newer systems allow companies to handle all others in the same manner, thus fully coordinating customer support resources.

Top-of-the-line customer service organizations also capture the conversation or e-mail data itself directly into the central database. This ensures accuracy and defensibility, which are critical requirements in industries like insurance or health care.

Customer self-service. Self-service functionality provides benefit to both the customer and the supplier by enhancing information available to the customer and by lowering the cost of interaction for the supplier. By giving customers online access to service or status information—the same information used internally—companies hope to build trust as well.

Partner Management Functions

Connection between "network leaders" and their partners is becoming easier and, with new capabilities for the communication of data using XML and Web services, it will become increasingly systematic. Currently, however, partner and supplier networks are mostly integrated the hard way—through electronic data interchange (EDI) and dedicated value-added networks.

In order to extend their network applications, suppliers try to persuade their partners to utilize a dedicated Web-based system to manage their sales and marketing activity.

Most companies have some problems integrating the information and procedures used for managing partners and those required for working with end customers. The scale of the problem can be significant, as companies like Cisco have found. Among other factors, a key problem Cisco encountered that led to its massive inventory write-down in 2001 was that its state-of-the-art Web-based partner site was not fully integrated with other systems and, as a result, it was possible to overstate demand for goods significantly. Cisco partners, in an effort to get their orders filled for the end users they served, would place two or three duplicate orders in the hope that at least some of the demand would be fulfilled. As demand dried up because of the rapid turnaround in the fortunes of dot-com companies, factories that were working to fill demand that was overstated found themselves with a massive excess.

What information is important to share? Most business-to-business companies share specific information on customer opportunities, sales history, and customer contact information. Consumer companies that work through distributors or retailers find it difficult to get to a level of individual customer demand today.

Full-support portal. Extending value to partners helps to motivate them as allies in your marketplace. Key information factors for motivating partners: knowledge and transactions. Providing partners with information on products, pricing, and other services with full access to corporate information helps to extend that feeling that they are integral to your cause. Of course, fluid, intuitive transaction capability ensures that your partners do not seek another organization that is easy to do business with.

Collaborative commerce. Collaboration at key points means that partners not only can access information but also can draw on the resources of their suppliers to create value for a mutual customer. For example, the creation or customization of a unique offering by a partner may require collaboration from an engineer or technician from the supplier.

Fully integrated workflow. The most important aspect of partner management may be the integration of managing sales opportunities and customer issues. In today's economy, partners and suppliers cannot afford to over- or undervalue their sales pipeline, nor can they afford to let customer issues fall through the cracks between them. Being fully informed of the steps taken by partners to win business and to solve customer issues is critical.

In order to do this, it only makes sense for partners to manage customer information through fully secure extranet-type applications that work on a limited portion of the main customer database.

Effective, new economy organizations understand that connecting with demand calls for extending their business and organizational architecture out into the network, not just the Internet but the increasingly interlinked customer ecosystem environment. In the earlier days of the Internet, technology architecture had limited capabilities, basically read-only, browser-based environments. The next generation was homogeneous transactional systems, which enabled interactions like transactions with customers. The coming new information standards, like UDDI (Universal Description, Discovery, and Integration) and XML, allow businesses for the first time to transact and to act in ways that they could never do before. They can leverage the Internet as a backbone to conduct business and, by leveraging these new standards, businesses can collaborate and deliver a much richer customer experience.

Through emerging Web services, companies will be able to use XML to encapsulate the data, to use the Simple Object Access Protocol (SOAP), which bundles its XML in a way that can be shipped across the Internet reliably to another business and shipped back. On top of that, the application of UDDI allows businesses to describe their interfaces so other businesses can transact with them. This is the beginning of truly distributed network computing. In order to use open information standards, Web services, and truly distributed computing, organizations will need to architect businesses that combine both technical and institutional design concepts.

For truly distributed network distributing to work in your organization, the key principles to understand and adopt are flexibility, open standards, change-enabled, modularity, accelerated, complexity, and individuated.

Visibility into Common Customer Data

For integrated customer relationship management to work, inroads must be made into a common language and structure for customer data. Like predecessor enterprise resource planning (ERP) implementations, the implementation of CRM has forced different groups—like sales, marketing, and customer service—to share information on customer service activities.

Subtle but important agreements on how to manage and adapt to street, town, and state name spellings provide a basis for enterprise-wide adoption of common data for understanding and influencing the external market environment.

As a first step in information integration, sharing sales, marketing, and customer service data initiates the dismantling of the "silos" created by functional organization structures—structures that, of course, have no place in an interdependent world of customer ecosystems.

Ensuring Flexibility

The only thing you can guarantee about current and future customers is that they're all different. For most companies, that means that they need to ensure that they can very rapidly deploy a customized solution. To do that we're going to need to have a very agile and flexible environment; we believe that Microsoft delivers that with the base, Windows 2000 platform, SQL Server, and the .NET Enterprise Servers. Without those, those solution families could not deliver the kind of customization with the speed and efficiencies we can today. Data management and storage processes will be different in many businesses, necessitating technical flexibility.

Organizational flexibility means creating capabilities for the different kinds of customer roles and the varied kinds of demand strategies outlined in the previous chapter. Flexibly deploying demand management engagement strategies means accepting that one size does not fit all customers!

Open Business Architecture

Organizational openness is more than open standards; it means looking for tools, techniques, and practices that bring customers closer to the center of your organization's core competence. Enabling customers to participate in change processes, whether incremental product improvement (like a quality assurance and testing program) or more radical change, requires a great deal of trust between customer and supplier.

Enabling open business architecture requires an understanding of the concept of "loose coupling." Integration of business systems among organizations in the past has meant that data feeds and integration protocols were tightly specified and purpose-built. Open standards for communicating data today and in the future mean that companies can communicate through information standards, with less effort to build and create new communications interfaces. It becomes much easier to start new relationships among customers, partners, and suppliers and, likewise, the perceived downside of ending a nonperforming relationship decreases.

Enabling this open architecture to work does require care and attention to security and privacy. For most companies, the balance between protecting the unique knowledge assets and sharing them through open architecture will be an ongoing challenge. The challenge will be both technical and organizational. Traditional logic is that a company does not share its core competencies with any other company. This concept will be challenged over the next few years, as collaboration among firms and customers will reach new levels. Quantum leaps in value creation will be enabled by the synergy among companies that carefully share competencies.

Change-Enabled

It's going to happen: computing and business design concepts are going to change. While right now the idea of a fully integrated e-business is seemingly the right thing for large-scale enterprises to do, fast on its tracks will be integration with the rest of the digital economy. Each computing paradigm has its share of hooks and snares, making it difficult to change in some fashion. We don't profess to be able to envision the future; we simply hope to enable organizations to adapt to it.

The concept of "change-enabled" also carries both institutional and technical connotations. The organizational architecture, that is, the processes and structures of a company, must be attuned to the potential for technical and process change. Most companies believe that they are more prepared to change than previous generations. Coping with ambiguity will be a critical skill for managers, executives, and employees in the network economy, because change will never quite be finished and organizations will still need to be productive.

Companies that survive massive software implementations, like the enterprise resource planning (ERP) implementations necessary for SAP and PeopleSoft applications, have been attuned to the need and the skills required to change the way their business works. Likewise, successful implementation of customer relationship management software has attuned organizations to the need to build business capability along with technology-enabled business process. Leading CRM experts argue that CRM is not about software, and they are correct—it's only half the equation.

So companies that have underachieved their objectives with CRM seek answers and new approaches to get value from their investment. As they recognize that attitudes and skills need to change, they ready their organization for another round of change.

The change required to adopt an enterprise demand management approach within a customer ecosystem is mostly a change in attitude, but it also involves a change in technology and organizational structure, as well as a shift in focus from business process to business capabilities.

Business and Application Modularity

As customer needs and market competition change, requirements for additional technological functionality emerge. Currently, content management, online selling, and online customer advisory services enhance online customer experiences, but there will be new functions and new capabilities down the road. In addition, it is clear that not all businesses will conduct the majority of their market and demand interactions online. For these kinds of networks, other capabilities are necessary, things like wireless and computer telephony capabilities that will work in the "bricks and mortar" businesses just as well as the "clicks and mortar" businesses.

Traditional business and technology architecture requires extensive planning and management to solve an organization's current problems. When a company acquires another company, a wrench is thrown into the works. The challenge of mergers and acquisitions is especially acute if a business's information architecture revolves around the primacy of a centralized database. A Web-services approach with loosely coupled, distributed database capability enables an organization to view its business units as modules of operation. It also enables the organization to add technology-enabled activity to extend business capabilities to customers and partners for resource synergy.

Note

1. As popularized through Seth Godin's book *Permission Marketing*. Permission marketing is, like many marketing concepts, applied liberally to simple activities related to opt-in email marketing, and thus not following the approach of a customer curriculum outlined by Godin.

6

Step 5: Turn Business Processes into Ecosystem Capabilities

Information technology is a critical tool for managing businesses today. But when it comes to managing customers and markets, most companies just don't get it right.

Companies in the hundreds or even the thousands have claimed failure with their e-marketing software or their customer relationship management software. While the answers are not simple, there are solutions available. The secret is to align technology so that it supports your ecosystem.

The most important part of that alignment is to look to the customer capabilities that are required directly and indirectly to support the relationship among all players that participate in the ecosystem. First, we will look at the idea of customer capabilities—the direct linkage of business skills with supporting information systems. Next, we will look at the specific capabilities needed to support a customer ecosystem. Finally, we will look at the specific functional tools that many companies have in place today and how to make use of them in the context of capabilities.

Create Customer Capabilities That Support the Customer Ecosystem

Many organizations have developed robust and sophisticated business processes for working with customers. In most companies, there are specific business processes that are automated, like the order entry process or the lead assignment process. As organizations and customers evolve, companies will need to evolve these processes into new and different configurations. As they do this, they will need to recognize that they need to create generic *customer capabilities* that will be distributed to partners, customers, and employees within their customer ecosystem.

Several similar concepts related to the concept of customer capabilities creating and leveraging internal sources of strategic advantage have been popularized, most with some degree of value. These concepts include business process, core competency, and activity systems. In this chapter we will refine the concept of *customer capabilities* that couples these similar notions of business competency with the idea of technology-enabled process or activity.

Creating Customer Capabilities

The concept of customer capabilities makes technology *strategic* in today's highly connected business world. By closely matching technology and business skills and resources, then distributing them to key points in a customer ecosystem, companies target resources and skills at the points of greatest leverage. Whether it is through channel or market partners, through their own online resources, or even directly to customers through wireless Web services, companies need to distribute generic demand capabilities to meet direct and indirect demand—where it occurs.

The basic concept of customer capabilities is composed of two elements: organizational competency and technology-enabled activity.

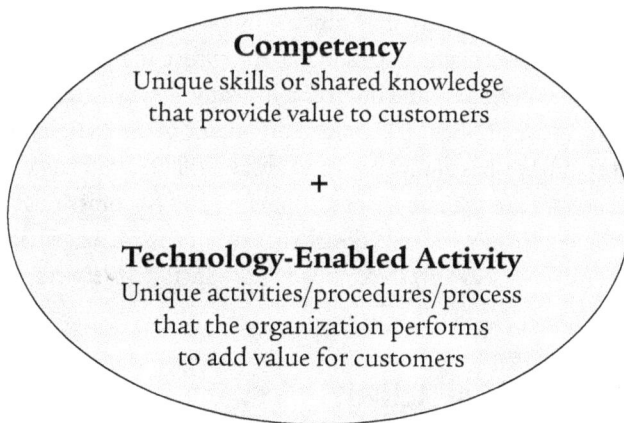

Competency
Unique skills or shared knowledge
that provide value to customers

+

Technology-Enabled Activity
Unique activities/procedures/process
that the organization performs
to add value for customers

Figure 6-1. Customer capabilities

Organizational Competency. Our perspective focuses on the common understanding that competencies are "what the organization is really good at," that is, the unique skills and qualities of an organization that set it apart from competitors. This may include unique knowledge or unique beliefs about how customers should be treated.

The concept of organizational capabilities is well known throughout academia and throughout executive offices. When business writers and consultants present concepts relating to business processes, capabilities, and competencies, they are essentially describing the same basic concept: the activities and knowledge that create value for customers. Our perspective is that some of these capabilities create "network-effect" value if they are creatively distributed directly to customers and partners to support a customer ecosystem. In order to better understand the idea, let us look at the origins of the capability concept in each of its component parts: process, competency, and activity.

Since the reengineering trend of the 1990s, the concept of business process has alternately been regarded with enthusiasm, derision, and ignorance. On the operations side of the business, process reengineering coupled with application integration has yielded spectacular results for some businesses and dismal failures for others. Yet the concept has had limited effect on the demand-creation side of the business. For some reason or set of reasons, marketers and sales and customer service organizations have largely ignored the concept of standardizing and reengineering their business processes.

The term "process" implies linearity and sequence. Perhaps because of this implication, marketing and sales people who are well aware that very little that they do is linear or repeatable in sequence resist the idea of process. The other issue, proven out over time, is that process improvement has mostly been an inward-focused exercise. Companies sought to improve the way things work for the benefit of the bottom line and often as a mask for downsizing.

From perspective of Michael Hammer, originator of the reengineering movement, however, process has always been and always will be about customers. "To a customer, processes are the essence of a company. The customer does not see or care about the company's organizational structure or its management philosophies .... The customer sees only the company's products and services, all of which are produced by its processes."[1]

Technology-Enabled Activity

Software runs many key activities in businesses today. Specific information related activities like creating a sales forecast, registering a transaction or creating a marketing opportunity report can be done solely buy human activity or with the support of technology. Technology-enabled activities represent an increasing component of how organizations create value. Activities, collectively grouped into processes, are the elements of an organization that create value by transforming inputs into something of value. According to Michael Porter, it is the underlying structure of activity systems that delivers true competitive advantage. Complex activity systems that uniquely are combined to create value represent the source of capability and the ultimate delivery of value to customers and unique advantage in the marketplace.

Weekly conference calls, monthly staff meetings, and other reporting activities shape the rhythm of interaction within an organization; these communications routines and reporting mechanisms provide a pulse that ensures that the work of the corporation is completed. A routine is composed of steps, expectations and formal or implied regularity. Automating the routines of an organization create reduced cost and improved quality, primarily. Most companies concentrate on the value of reducing the cost of a process by enabling the activity with some from of technology

It is often the more abstract activities that create the most strategic value for companies. Directing how customer problems get solved, for example, may have been an random or individual-directed process in the past, but because it is directed by software and communications technology, the undefined organizational skill is now copied throughout an organization.

Customer Interaction Capabilities

Effectively linking with ecosystem demand means that an organization must be able to link with the core relationships—customer, partner, and influencer—in a way that is appropriate and adds value to the shared relationship objectives. Current thinking about relationships is that the company should just provide whatever means of interaction medium is desired by the stakeholder: phone, fax, Web, wireless, and so on. The company must be able to manage and control relationships with customers, partners, stakeholder communities, and other demand influencers in a dynamic environment.

Customer interaction capabilities are the key organizational skills that are required to compete effectively in the demand driven economy. They link the necessary functions with the necessary technology to manage relationships in multiple channels.

Servicing. Organizations need to have procedures and routines for responding to incoming communications regarding products or services that they have already

	Personalizing	Transacting	Servicing	Fulfilling
Organizational Competency	Develop relevant approaches to personalization	Manage, coordinate multiple modes of transaction Innovate transaction systems	Conceive and deliver quality service	Conceive standards for fulfillment, innovation in fulfillment strategy, fulfillment comple-ments whole customer experience
Technology-Enabled Activity	Flexible, adaptive interfaces in various media	Reliable, seamless capture of transaction data Secure, trustworthy transaction systems	Capture service requirement Manage service process	System linkage to physical delivery infrastructure

Figure 6–2. Generic customer interaction capabilities

sold. They can maintain the customer as asset through effective approaches to solving problems and to providing information about orders or other issues. Effective support and service process needs to be broken down further into sub-processes and activities.

Companies that successfully link the support and service processes with the demand-generation processes are also the ones that are most successful with customer lifetime value and customer loyalty.

The most obvious example of servicing capabilities is frequently asked questions or self-diagnostics available through the Internet. By linking the questions asked by customers most often, organizations put their knowledge in front of customers, unhampered by the influence of what was asked most recently or with the most insistence.

Servicing: Capabilities in the Customer Ecosystem

Online
- Support management capability is extended to users through software, enabling customers to make inquiries, search for resolutions, and solve issues on their own.

Offline
- Internal users have same access to customer support information and functionality. Enhanced capabilities allow them to service more advanced needs.

Distributed
- Partners and dealers have capability to service customers within similar time requirements.

Companies that support the service capability with rigorous incident management and organizations will have a fact-based linkage of the skill and the technology-enabled activity.

Transacting. The capability of evaluating, prioritizing, and advancing business leads and opportunities is the critical capability to capitalize on value creation. The requirement for managing business opportunity may be straightforward and direct in some industries, such as in the retail sector, but in other business sectors, this process is the most critical, the most varied, and the most dependent on individual skill. There is no hiding it, despite the complex interactions and myriad forms of partnering: in the end being demand driven means creating revenue. This means that it is also all about making a transaction happen. Enabling, recording, linking, and streamlining the transaction are key elements of the interaction capability.

Confusion often arises about the definition of "sales process" in an organization. For most companies, it is probably the simplest of all, involving the advancement of a potential customer from the lead or suspect level to the prospect stage and finally to customer status. While this is perhaps the most documented part of demand management processes, it is probably the most variable and potentially the most misunderstood.

Acquiring leads for new business opportunities has been one of the most intensively examined processes in the marketing discipline. Network-based businesses must think of the other relationships as well, such as partners, influencers, and consultants. While it is critical to define the activities that a company will use

---

Transacting: Capabilities in the Customer Ecosystem

Online
+ Online transactions, enabled for multichannel, multimedia capabilities

Offline
+ Organizational competency and technology-enabled activity to manage through selling cycle to transaction
+ Capability to manage multiple modes of transaction and link to operational systems

Distributed
+ Transaction capability extended to partners in flexible manner that continues to support customer experience
+ Competency and activity to manage selling process

---

in this process, it is also important to enable flexibility in the processes. In many organizations, this process requires constant change, as new and hopefully better sources of relationships.

New Internet communications standards such as UDDI will enable the acquisition of potential customer and supplier relationships to be conducted more efficiently and effectively online. Thus, the organization or institutional element of this part of the process will change in emphasis from a mechanistic, labor-intensive task to one of fluid social or interpersonal relationship building, depending on the customer's value orientation.

Formulating transaction capabilities from the market and demand perspective provides insights not possible from an accounting or operational perspective. For example, Amazon.com's "one-click" transaction management process is not a critical supply chain concept; it is most definitely a customer and ecosystem management concept. Accounting and supply chain perspectives would help to ensure that a transaction works and that it's secure, but not necessarily that it's easy.

Fulfilling. Is distribution and fulfillment a customer ecosystem capability? It is perhaps simply a matter of perspective. For example, if you are the customer and you have a high level of control over your supplier, you may have the supply chain perspective. If, however, you are the supplier seeking to provide fulfillment capabilities that differentiate you from your competitors, you may wish to view distribution and fulfillment from the demand management perspective.

Fulfilling: Capabilities in the Customer Ecosystem

Online
- Tracking/monitoring of fulfillment status distributed to customers

Offline
- Planning and problem-solving skills coupled with technology tools
- Customization/personalization options developed and enabled

Distributed
- Partners participate in fulfillment planning and are enabled to provide services
- Customization/personalization fulfillment technology distributed to partners

---

Another aspect of the fulfillment capabilities is that this is the primary linkage of the left and right brain of the organization, of the supply and demand management perspectives. This is a critical linkage for most companies, because it enables product customization based on personalization requirements. The provision of effective fulfillment capabilities in the customer ecosystem that respond to customer requirements in a flexible adaptive manner can provide a unique advantage over competitors.

The tracking of packages for delivery is a key capability for major delivery companies like FedEx and UPS. They have not only built the technology to support fulfillment, but also linked it closely to organizational skill. Furthermore, by distributing the technology to partners like contract shippers and specialty logistics partners, they enable the entire ecosystem to completely participate.

Personalizing. Personalization is emerging as a basic customer service requirement in the information age. Much of the technology available for personalization offers simple cosmetic changes for an interface. Although customers respond somewhat to this entry-level form of personalization capability, much more is possible. With product configuration applications, a company can provide its customers with the ability to create their own specific combinations of product attributes or combinations of services that meet their particular needs in real time.

Personalizing: Capabilities in the Customer Ecosystem

Online
- Modification of customer interfaces, meaningful change of content or context depending on customer roles

Offline
- Effective linkage to production processes
- Determine appropriate personalization strategies, e.g., cosmetic personalization (changing only the way information is presented) or adaptive personalization (changing both the presentation and the content)

Distributed
- Support and extend the personalized relationship through technology to partners

---

The challenge for most companies is to make the inside match the outside. That is, while many companies can provide the customers with a long list of options from which to choose, they cannot always deliver on these choices.

The most common examples of companies that are using personalization technology are using it for cosmetic purposes only; Yahoo!, MSN, and other portal sites are using personalization to enable individuals to organize information. The linkage of organizational capability for personalization to technology remains more difficult to achieve. The key challenge is linking specific information about individual customers to your offering or business. Financial services companies, for example, continue to deal with segments of customers rather than individuals; that's why you continue to receive generic offers from a credit card company that you already do business with. The excuse the company will use is that the customer acquisition function is provided by a third party. This statement, however, is simply proof that it has not distributed the personalization capability to its partners.

Customer Ecosystem Positioning Capabilities

Al Ries and Jack Trout identified the concept of positioning as the "battle for the mind" in the world of business.[2] Positioning has primarily been an outbound marketing communications concern.

Many companies that have deployed contact management, sales force automation, and customer relationship management software complain that the software installation has not yielded the insights on markets and customers that were promised. In our experience, many companies fall into the fatal trap of equating a software application's promised capability with their organizations' capability to deliver. In few other areas is it so apparent as with *customer learning* and *market sensing* that customer management software has failed to live up to its promise.

Why is this? There are many, many reasons why most companies fail to fully utilize the information that they have at their fingertips.

The process of learning about demand is complex and varies greatly among organizations. It often falls through the cracks in terms of responsibility among

	Understanding	Engaging	Adapting	Influencing
Organizational Competency	Ability/orientation for understanding markets and customers	Orientation to build involvement with customers	Ability to balance demand creation with demand responsiveness Readiness to co-opt the best staff leverage technology for constant change	Understanding and facility with the broad set of inter-relationships among companies
Technology-Enabled Activity	Data collection and disseminaton	Customer relationship management software and systems	Customization/ evolution of product/service offering Customization/ evolution of business systems for customers and partners	Partner relationship management software Content management Product configuration, suggestive systems

Figure 6-3. Generic ecosystem positioning capabilities

the customer-facing functions. Proactive roles and activities, like market analysis or research, are often the first to be cut in more difficult economic conditions.

In order to be effective in managing information and turning it into organizational knowledge, firms must leverage the newly available technologies with processes and attitudes. Three main process elements—framing and definition, inquiry and information collection, and interpretation and dissemination—provide a nonsequential framework for learning about the business environment.

Understanding. Understanding customers and markets in a complex business environment is one of the most elusive capabilities for companies. It seems that few have mastered the right combination of competency and technology-enabled activity. The tremendous explosion of variety and volume of information resources available through the Internet and other services ultimately worsens the problem.

Understanding: Capabilities in the Customer Ecosystem

Online
- ◆ Capable of gathering rich data through customer interfaces

Offline
- ◆ Able to gather and sort data from many sources, supplementing online customer data
- ◆ Frame, define, and disseminate information and knowledge about customers within the organization

Distributed
- ◆ Gather information requirements from partners
- ◆ Extend understanding of customers to partners for mutual benefit

---

From a competency perspective, organizations need to frame and define the information they need. Ensuring that information is of some value is a critical process requirement in this age of information overload. The critical element of the framing and definition stage is the element of time and timing. Framing and definition are too often carried out as ad hoc practices when management, marketing, or sales executives are out in search of an answer to a specific problem. Market and customer research is commissioned to deal with a problem or a specific question is asked of the sales force.

Technology implementation has been seen as cure-all for addressing strategic issues like customer relationship management. Massive data warehouses with incredible data access tools should be able to solve the problem of understanding customers. It is interesting to note that while *data mining* is regarded as an important technology breakthrough from the technologist's perspective, it is a term that is used with mild derision in research circles because it is taken to imply that the research and analysis is actually directionless and of uncertain value—mining to see what is there, rather than having a plan or even a hypothesis.

Yet, most companies are accustomed to ongoing financial reports that provide information about the companies' past performance. Customer relationship management databases can offer some perspective as leading indicators, provided that the questions are framed correctly.

Periodic data collection may remain expensive and complex, but more and more companies have access to extensive customer data through internal systems. As mentioned earlier, contact management systems are often implemented with the promise of bringing insight into customer behavior through extensive data availability. The challenge of the day is to ensure that data is useful and relevant for the key issues facing the business.

Information sources from the Internet can provide in-context information about potential customers and partners. Companies can filter public information using emerging standards and leverage it on a regular basis with less and less effort.

Interpretation of customer and market data can be disseminated through *mental models*. George Day defines "mental models" as "simplifying frameworks used to make sense of the world and keep the organization moving in a common direction."[3] A good example of a mental model is the following assertion from American Medical Security Group (AMS): "Consumers depend on independent agents to help make decisions."[4] This mental model underpins many of the company's decisions about how to go to market. Decisions about which products to offer and through which channels are made on the basis of the widely held belief about consumer dependence on independent agents.

Unchallenged mental models can be a source of potential business failure. As Day points out, they can become traps. If, for example, AMS continued to believe that the independent agent route is unimpeachable, while its competitors are providing more and more services directly on the Internet, yet still compensating the independent agent, AMS may find its market position eroded.

Technology, such as an intranet, enables companies to share information, but to share *knowledge*, companies need competency and culture to help enable the interpretation of information in context so that it becomes knowledge. Data-mining and intelligence software tools are critical to creating and extracting new pieces of information, but sharing information and, more important, knowledge is a far greater challenge.

Information sharing between ecosystem partner organizations is critical to building trust in the mutual relationship. It begins with sharing information through secure Internet applications that provide both parties with critical transactional information. Other information provided could include support and training information. But this is merely information.

Sharing knowledge is a greater challenge. Smaller organizations, simply because of scale differences, can mistrust larger firms. Partners of equal size may mistrust one another because of diverging objectives for their common customer. Requirements for the customer-linking process, such as aggressiveness and customer bonding, may conflict with the knowledge-building process by deterring openness.

Engaging. For many years, the software industry called the technology-enabled part of this capability "contact management." Changes in customer roles, the increased control capability of customers and range of relationships, and the range of tools and techniques for engaging with all kinds of contacts have broadened the scope of need for both competency and technology-enabled activity.

Engaging in the Customer Ecosystem

Online
- Capable of providing unique interfaces that engage in many modes and appeal to many senses

Offline
- Capable of capturing demand consistently in various modes

Distributed
- Enabled to support experience through partners

Of course, the nature of engagement should be relevant to your customers' preferred roles and to their control orientation. Customer engagement activities, at a high level, are generic among companies. In reality, however, the ways that companies link with their customers will vary dramatically. Nonetheless, there are some standard requirements for relationship tracking, such as:

- The ability to track interactions through telephone, fax, e-mail, and Web inquiry and to do so virtually automatically.
- The ability to automate interaction events, such as follow-up calls or renewal inquiries, based on customer satisfaction or business development objectives.
- The ability to coordinate the tracking of all relationships, not just key customers or key partners. Tracking customer and partner relationships in dif-

ferent business systems or not tracking partner relationships will provide a company with only part of the customer ecosystem equation.

In a complex ecosystem, different customer segments and different customer roles are driven by different variables. One segment of a business may have direct sales relationships, while other parts of the business may depend heavily on intermediary relationships. This is the very essence of many-to-many marketing relationships. Tracking the nature of many relationships regardless of where they might occur is a core process for a network business. For example, the ultimate buyer may purchase directly from a manufacturer or supplier online, but the partner that built the personal, offline relationship will still need to know about the purchase. Otherwise, the breakdown of relationship between manufacturer and partner may provide an erroneous view of where to deploy assets or how to leverage network assets.

In simpler terms, this capability represents all the communications activities a company will require for all of the various stakeholders in its broad demand arena. Coordination of communications is increasingly network-based and increasingly converging. Ensuring effective coverage of communications requirements to shareholders, partners, customers, and other intermediaries is primarily about ensuring that technology is utilized most effectively. Included in this capability are the market communications planning cycle and other relevant marketing communications processes.

Adapting. If you accept that companies need to be more flexible and more fluid in their response to demand patterns, also accept that business strategy must be responsive and fluid as well. Most companies are fortunate to have a strategic plan that at least gives them direction. At the risk of complicating their business process exceedingly, we offer some core processes for designing a fluid, responsive, demand driven organization.

Many companies have periodic strategic planning process. While planning may be too rigid for the dynamic and complex customer ecosystems of today, the process for evaluating changes in the business is still valuable. Three essential issues need to be reviewed in the process:

- ◆ It almost goes without saying that companies regularly must assess market-driven changes; companies need to make sense of the changes in customer needs, wants, and attitudes, in competitor and partner positioning, and in overall market change.
- ◆ With increasing frequency, companies must have a process for assessing whether technology changes require new approaches to the market or to their business architecture.

Adapting: Capabilities in the Customer Ecosystem

Online
- Fluid response to understanding
- Capable of real change to offering beyond personalization

Offline
- Dynamic response to market and customer understanding
- Ability to reconfigure capabilities and business activities as determined through strategic decisions, market needs

Distributed
- Able to reorganize partnerships to work with changing demand forces
- Able to change extended partner activity rapidly

- Changes in organizational priorities are inevitable, as are changes in key personnel.

In developing business systems for managing business relationships, there are two distinct beliefs about designing and implementing the business information system: one is that if a system already exists that performs basic functions and processes, just adopt the business system and processes and run with it; and the other is that if it's going to work here, it had better fit the way we want to do business.

The activities that a company undertakes to deliver value and to manage customers are critical to its competitive position. Duplicating another company's customer management processes or customer support or its knowledge and value creation processes is to admit that you have nothing unique to offer in terms of relationship. Best practices in some areas of business process may be possible, especially in the area of manufacturing or logistics, but in the area of demand network relationships, each company will have nuances and unique ways of doing business. Adapting technology to ensure uniqueness is a prerequisite for success.

Excellence in managing and adapting organizational capabilities is enabled by ensuring that your best people participate in the design, not only of strategy, but also of activity and change. Frequently, application design is left to technical specialists who may or may not know the core activities or central "reason for being" of the corporation. Top-performing companies keep top performers involved with designing activities even if it costs in the short term. We have heard countless stories of companies unhappy with the design of their business process or business application, but unwilling to take the time to invest up front to ensure strategic fit.

In contrast, we have seen top performers raise the level of all staff by using automation and technology to improve overall performance.

An excellent example of this is RBC Dain Rauscher, a Wall Street investment bank, which temporarily assigned several top revenue earners to a software implementation project designed to create new customer management processes. Many companies would consider that the cost of these top earners being off their core function would be unnecessary or even impractical. The payoff of this knowledge sharing is a business architecture that truly reflects corporate knowledge assets. RBC Dain Rauscher's return on this investment was rapid and significant, discussed more fully in Chapter 9.

With many CRM projects in the past, the completion of the project was seen as the accomplishment. Companies have mastered the idea that new projects lead to change in the business organization and that new technology is often critical in making that change. But for many the challenge is the transition from project to ingrained routine.

Developing business objectives: Many change projects and particularly information technology projects are developed with some vague idea that the technology will enable the company to do something new. For example, a company adopts a new customer management system so that it can target more effectively. At the outset, it has no specific concept of what segments it needs to target more effectively, nor does it have a specific goal in mind for the business to benefit from the investment of time and money.

Disseminating vision and direction: Business change projects often require the leadership and direction of a champion and a sponsor, who develop specialized knowledge and skill. The project is technically successful, but because the champion has created a unique capability or skill he or she becomes quite valuable on the open market and leaves. Shortly thereafter, the impact of this project and its vision dissipates.

Influencing. A customer ecosystem involves a complex series of interactions that result in business transactions. The role of the ecosystem technology is to support and respond to demand in whatever forms (direct or indirect). It is also serves to create and channel demand for goods, services, and experience that an organization may work to provide.

For all involved, the endgame is a transaction with a customer that believes an offering is worth an amount of money that is more than what it cost the provider to assemble it, an endgame no different from what has been occurring for eons.

This set of demand-influencing capabilities enables companies to link to

> ## Influencing: Capabilities in the Customer Ecosystem
>
> **Online**
> - Able to influence demand through messaging systems and messaging strategy
>
> **Offline**
> - Able to influence structure of markets and partners through broad-scale activities
>
> **Distributed**
> - Able to extend consistent customer experience through partners
> - Able to extend information on customer needs to partners

more complex customers and networks, to learn about them, and to change rapidly to ensure that their offerings continue to provide value.

Our earlier discussion of how Microsoft distributed influence around the NT server business is an example of how a company can distribute influence throughout a customer ecosystem, directly by communicating with customers and indirectly through partners. Although this example may hold less weight because of tough times in the networking equipment sector, Cisco has been effective in distributing influence directly to customers and indirectly to partners through highly developed Internet systems.

Linking Capabilities with Adaptive Strategy Ensures the Smart Use of Technology

The smart use of technology and of organizational capabilities in a customer ecosystem occurs because companies emphasize the right skills for the right strategies. The following section gives a rough guideline on the primary capabilities for the key adaptive strategies for building and responding to customer ecosystem dynamics:

1. **Build Influence and Engagement Capability and Technology for Promotion Strategies**

   Companies that are trying to create demand with promotional strategies will need to build technology to distribute influence and enable close engagement with customers. The primary skills and capabilities for influencing customers are outward-oriented.

2. **Reconfigure Ecosystems with Influence and Adaptation**

   Reconfiguring an ecosystem requires that companies move the balance of power away from the customer to a greater degree of shared control. The two main sets of capabilities used for these sets of strategies are influence and adaptation.

3. **Using Interaction Capabilities to Rapidly React to Customers**
The emphasis in reaction strategies is on the transaction capabilities of fulfillment, service, and transaction. To some extent, the capabilities to maintain rapport and contact with customers are also necessary, so engagement is necessary but secondary. Investing in personalization may be of some benefit if it enables more effective reaction.

4. **Enabling Effective Exchange with Customers Through Interaction Capabilities**
Where customers are primarily activists, companies need to emphasize capabilities to interact effectively. It will be beneficial for suppliers to enable their customers to personalize and take control of many aspects of the business interaction.

5. **Facilitating Collaborative Strategies with a Full Slate of Customer Capabilities**
As expected, collaborative strategies require the full range of technology for positioning and interaction. This is the most challenging of all positions in a marketplace.

Although we have described the primary capabilities above, the transaction capabilities for responding to demand are, for the most part, required for all adaptive strategies as identified in the Figure 6-4.

	Positioning Capabilities	Interaction Capabilities
Promote	Influence, Engage	Fulfill, Service, Transact
Reconfigure	Influence, Adapt, Engage	Fulfill, Service, Transact
React	Engage	Fulfill, Service, Transact
Exchange	Understand, Adapt	Fulfill, Service, Transact, Personalize
Collaborate	Engage, Adapt, Understand, Influence	Fulfill, Service, Transact, Personalize

Figure 6-4. Adaptive strategies

Notes

1. Michael Hammer, *Beyond Reengineering* (New York: HarperBusiness, 1996), p. 12.
2. Al Ries and Jack Trout, *Positioning: The Battle for Your Mind* (New York: McGraw-Hill, 1969).
3. George S. Day, *The Market Driven Organization* (New York: Free Press, 1999), p. 93.
4. Paraphrase of interview comment from Mark Seghers of American Medical Security Group.

7

Step 6: Synchronize Your Customer Ecosystem and Supply Chain

T he ability to cope with uncertainty and complexity on the customer-facing side of the business can mean the difference between reaching revenue and profit targets and falling far short. Ensuring that supply responds to changes in demand—essential to avoid costly unusable inventory. The need for synchronizing customer ecosystem and supply chain goes far beyond getting marketing and sales and manufacturing staff to acknowledge their different worldviews.

What can be done to synchronize the customer ecosystem and the supply chain? The most successful organizations are able to integrate adaptive, complexity-based thinking into their supply chain as well as more structure and control into their customer ecosystem. For example, the rapid growth of biotech market leader, Biogen, was predicated on its ability to respond to a rapid growth in demand through an adaptive channel of distribution that was fundamentally different from existing supply chains in the pharmaceutical sector.

Many issues are outside the control of the organization, occurring in the market or with customers. Some of the key issues that make it difficult to match demand and supply include:

- ◆ **Short product lifecycle.** In today's markets, consumer, technical, and otherwise, market opportunities may be fast and fleeting. Products like toys and consumer electronics need to be constantly revamped and revised in order to keep customers upgrading and coming back. What customers demand today may not be in the supply chain, which may be full of products that customers don't want.
- ◆ **Unpredictable demand creation.** Old promotion techniques have less and less effect on a jaded, empowered consumer. Advertising programs have progressively less and less result in creating new markets. Yet, seemingly spontaneously, new demand can arise from word of mouth or stimulated word-of-mouth marketing programs.
- ◆ **Seasonality.** Seasonal demand is a challenge for many organizations. Intrawest Corporation, for example, must deal with seasonal demand for many of its winter sports properties. Like many ski resort companies, it has tried to counter the seasonality factor by establishing summer sports like golf and tennis as part of its resort facilities.
- ◆ **Partner demand forecast uncertainty.** Despite the many advantages of partners in demand creation, one major drawback remains—due to separate information systems or procedures, the forecast of demand from partners may not emerge as your partners believe.

Demand-Side Skills

There are some skills linked with technology that will enable better synchronization of demand and supply. As discussed in the earlier chapter on capabilities, there are certain generic capabilities that need to be emphasized in synchronizing supply and demand. By emphasizing positioning-type generic capabilities and leveraging their organizational skills with the appropriate technology, companies can have more effective control over demand and over demand variability in particular (see Figure 7-1).

Methodology-Based Forecasting

How can demand forecasting get better? Most demand forecasts depend on the intuition of sales and marketing managers and their frontline staff. For both managers and sales representatives, forecasting is a hit-and-miss business. Lack of knowledge of customer intentions, market conditions, and unforeseen, uncontrollable pressures make it practically impossible for frontline staff to forecast demand accurately.

Customer Ecosystem Issue	Generic Capability	Enterprise Demand Management Technique or Tool
Short Product Lifecycle	Influence	Rapid Product Cycling
Uncertain Market Creation	Influence + Understanding	Market Testing
Seasonality	Influence + Adaptation	Product Cycling Flexible Pricing Systems
Fluctuating Product Demand	Understanding	Methodology-Based Forecasting
Partner Demand Forecasting Uncertainty	Understanding	Integrated Opportunity Management

Figure 7-1. Customer issues and positioning capabilities

Linking sales process and standardized sales steps to demand evaluation through technology enhances an organization's competency at understanding demand. By standardizing the rating for a potential sale, rather than leaving forecasts to subjective estimates, companies can develop greater consistency among sales reps.

Rapid Product Cycling

Ever notice how effective Mattel and Hasbro are at continually finding new products to capture the attention of youngsters and revenue from parents? Companies in the toy industry have learned how to deal with the very short pre-Christmas sales season and the very short fad cycles inherent in toys.

Companies that have to deal with short product lifecycles need to focus on improving supply responsiveness, as well as influencing change in their customer ecosystem.

Rapid product cycling can help to create new demand as well as to address existing demand. Rapidly cycling product generations can enable the company to signal to the market to anticipate new products or new versions. For many years, Gap's six-week product season enabled rapid turnover of inventory as well as giving customers the indication that something new would be happening every few weeks, giving them some reason to visit the store again. Gap's portfolio of standard products, along with continually changing new style and color programs, gave it the ability to both create and respond to customer needs, albeit within a fairly narrow range of fashion taste. As its core market has moved more dramatically away from its core offering, Gap has not really shown an ability to make more radical changes to core products and services.

Rapid cycling of product assortment can create an image of collectibility. Beanie Babies, a popular collectible as much as a popular toy made by Ty, Inc., were changed on a much more rapid basis than traditional doll-type products. Rather than having an entire year's or season's assortment available at once, the company shipped new assortments monthly or more frequently, giving collectors a reason to continue to check with retailers for new items.

Market Testing

Another lesson from toy distributors is the ability to use online or distributed capabilities to test and adapt to demand before a product or service is launched.

Distributed transaction capabilities, specifically Web-based and partner-based transaction systems, make it possible to test market demand much more easily. For example, for the launch of the new Xbox video game console by Microsoft, Toys "R" Us presold packages of the gaming system along with peripherals in advance of the launch date from its toysrus.com Web site. The retailer's entire first allotment was sold out in 30 minutes. The prelaunch sale achieved the critical aim of reducing the risk of a new product launch. Advance forecasting of this demand was exactly matched to the supply that it needed to purchase.

Advance testing of product demand is possible for more than just consumer products. Technology products such as software, hardware, and telecom products are often preannounced for market communications purposes. The difficulty is that many of these products are pushed, rather than pulled, into the customer eco-system.

Flexible Pricing

Lands' End, the catalog retailer, has successfully transitioned its business to include an online storefront. Standard pricing in its catalog and main online store is held for new introductions for a period of time and for standard product offerings in general. Depending on stock levels and selling patterns of products, seasonal or specialty goods may be featured in an overstock section. From there, products that are still in oversupply will go into a reverse auction, with the price going down every few days until all the supply is sold off.

Pricing as a mechanism to synchronize demand and supply is a great opportunity for companies. Leading industry analysts and futurists like Don Tapscott argue that organizations must be prepared to "define the price-discovery mechanism, not the price."[1]

Dynamic, flexible pricing is a threat for traditional marketing, to be sure, but a new way for companies to gain acceptance for openness and fairness in an ecosystem. The most prominent example of dynamic pricing is eBay, of course, but this is an entirely new business model designed for peer-to-peer or business-to-consumer markets.

From a distributed capabilities perspective, flexible pricing is all about adaptation. In terms of how small and mid-sized companies can use flexible pricing to adapt to market demand, the most effective and easiest technique will likely be to sell some of their offerings through online marketplaces. The entrepreneurial firm thus relies on the capabilities of its partners to adapt to market demand through flexible pricing.

Integrated Opportunity Management

As we mentioned earlier, one of Cisco's major challenges prior to its massive inventory write-down was a lack of visibility into the individual demand for its routers and switches ordered through value-added resellers. While Cisco is recognized as an absolute leader in most distributed technology capabilities, it appears the company experienced a hiccup in its ability to forecast and respond to end-customer orders—a $2 billion hiccup.

One of the key culprits, apart from a supply chain that did not shut down immediately, was a partner opportunity management system that was not able to capture demand at an individual customer level. Demand from partners was identified by a named client business deal or named business opportunity, giving Cisco the sense that it was able to account for all the specific orders in the customer ecosystem. However, it seems that it was not able to account for customers that ordered from more than one specific partner and that might order double or triple the volume of product that they needed in order to compensate for the lags in delivery and lack of assurance.

In order to improve the reliability of customer demand forecasts, Cisco and other companies have moved to integrate partner forecasts and customer forecasts. Increasingly companies are deploying a single, Web-enabled database that houses individual customer information tied to reseller or retailer information. Demand and opportunity forecasts are thus more easily assessed at an individual level.

Supply-Side Responsiveness

A basic belief of supply chain management practitioners is that customer demand forecasts are just not reliable. Salespeople pad their forecasts to impress sales management, customers never complete their orders as they say they will, and there is a general lack of rigor in forecasts from any third parties. As a result, serious supply chain folks will look at demand forecasts with more than a little skepticism. Responsive supply chain tactics are thus critical to gear up the supply machinery to fulfill demand. The manufacturing management response is to reduce cycle times in all key processes and to adopt flexible manufacturing to ensure that production can rapidly respond to changes in varieties and quantities demanded.

Supply Chain Paradigm	Customer Ecosystem Drivers	Examples
Virtual Supply Chain	Rapid Unpredictable Growth	Cisco, Nortel
Distributed Supply Chain Planning	Distributed Customer Fulfillment Capabilities	CPFR, Nabisco, Wegmans
Supply Re-intermediation	Influence Capabilities	Biogen
Build to Order	Personalization Capabilities	Dell, General Motors, Atlas Copco

Figure 7-2. Technology and supply-side responsiveness

For many years, especially in the high-tech industry, a key strategy to create supply-chain responsiveness has been the virtual supply chain. Outsourcing of key production activities to third parties, according to the likes of Nortel and Cisco, was the panacea for all supply chain challenges. In addition, the asset leverage that we promote on the customer-facing side of the business was also achievable and desirable on the production side of a virtual business.

Virtual Supply Chain

The virtual supply chain was supposed to be flexible and scalable, both in terms of response to increased demand and in backing off from declining demand. What companies like Cisco and a host of others have tried to do is outsource their manufacturing to a group of specialist, high-tech manufacturers.

Cisco's virtual approach to manufacturing is based on outsourcing manufacturing of not just non-core parts or assemblies, but entire products and product lines, because of critical advantages:

- Specialization of the contract manufacturers leads to economies of scale and "learning curve" advantages that provide ultimate value to customers.
- Scalability of contract requirements were intended to create a response.
- Inventory is reduced because contract manufacturers could pool parts requirements of similar items, such as components and boxes.
- Leverage assets, by utilizing capital for acquiring technology, people, and market potential, as opposed to production capacity as traditional manufacturers have done. In the heyday of the Internet bubble, return on invested capital for Cisco was about twice that of competitors like Nortel and Lucent.[3]

Interestingly, some market watchers note that, even in times of contraction, this approach appears to provide the promised advantages. Unfortunately, it cannot prevent the pain or surprise that comes with a market reversal.

Distributed Supply Chain Planning

As businesses combine and subdivide in the demand driven economy, the viability of centralized planning of inventory, distribution, production, and other supply chain functions decreases. But it may not disappear entirely in the short term.

Even with scanner-based point-of-sales systems, demand forecasts suffer from a lack of rigor and relevance. As we often witness, a cashier will scan three products in the same family, even though they may be of different colors or flavors, in order to speed the checkout process. Accordingly, inventory levels in a retail store will very often be financially accurate but on an item-by-item basis completely incorrect. Retail forecasters are left with incorrect data to build product-level forecasts. The retailer, the manufacturer, and the distributor are left depending on a forecast built on the best assessment by staff rather than on unassailably accurate data.

Distributed supply chain planning is rapidly becoming more popular, owing to the Collaborative Planning, Forecasting and Replenishment (CPFR) initiative started by consumer goods industry players, including retailers like Wal-Mart and Wegmans (a major grocery retailer) and consumer products manufacturers like Nabisco Brands and Procter & Gamble. This initiative, established in 1998, has rapidly gained popularity for its ability to provide simultaneous benefit. Research indicates that the standards established by the initiative have increased sales by as much as 80% between partners, while yielding inventory reductions of at least 10%.[4] Other benefits include improved inventory availability (i.e., fill rates), which results in greater goods available for sale, and more rapid inventory turns, which provide more efficient use of working capital.

Distribution Innovation

If you can remove or renovate some steps in the supply chain to shift risk or responsibility, to reduce time or cost of moving products from manufacturer to consumer, you may have re-intermediated supply. A strange term perhaps for supply chain re-engineering, but basically it means that, in certain cases, shifting warehousing activities or delivery or inventory stocking responsibility may improve your ability to synchronize supply and demand.

Traditional supply chains may simply be too inflexible or costly to meet with an expected rapid rise in demand. Biogen, a biotechnology research company, found itself in this enviable position when its breakthrough formulation for multiple sclerosis, Avonex, appeared certain to receive FDA approval in mid-1995. But as a research house, Biogen had only the capability to manufacture the drug, not to package, warehouse, or distribute.[5]

Ensuring that it had the key capabilities to support the demand side of the equation together required Biogen to work closely with its chosen partners. In particular, it focused on:

- Placing Biogen staff at partner locations to support launch and ramp-up planning through training and supervision
- Providing a comprehensive information system to share production, warehousing, and distribution data
- Setting standards of service and responsiveness to focus on meeting the perceived avalanche of demand

The dramatic benefits of the product over existing treatments helped to propel the demand for Avonex in very rapid fashion. Within six months, it had surpassed the existing treatment and captured 60% of the market.

Build to Order

When Rogers and Peppers popularized one-to-one marketing, they linked it to mass customization and build-to-order manufacturing strategies. One cannot assume that mass customization and build-to-order are synonymous.

The basic premise of the build-to-order concept is to remove forecasting from the supply process altogether. Like the very successful Dell Computer that assembles in a matter of days complete PCs, servers, or notebooks only upon the receipt of an order and usually full payment, all manners of companies are striving to complete full assembly of all required parts of a product only when a complete customer commitment is received. The phenomenal success of this model in computers has caught the eye of companies in other, more capital-intensive industries, like automobile manufacturing, for its ability to minimize the carrying cost of finished goods inventory and to maximize customer satisfaction by the ability to tailor products to individual tastes.

Central to this concept is speeding the process of configuring products through fully integrated product configuration systems. Configuration systems can be utilized to smooth the process of relating demand to supply, not only at a high level for the finished product, but also cascaded down into the component parts that are required for the end product.

Specifications and design requirements for rock face drilling equipment tend to be very unique. Atlas Copco, as a US$5 billion global supplier of industrial products, from pneumatic hand tools to rig-mounted drifting assemblies, with head offices in Stockholm, Sweden, contends with the unique challenges of building the right product for very specific requirements for each customer each and every day.

In the past, the process of building the right product was cumbersome. Typically, a sales representative would speak to the customer, getting information on how to meet their requirements. Then, the sales representative would access information from a range of information systems and, if not available locally, get the document from another location. Product or order information would be returned to the customer by fax or courier. After that, modifications could take several iterations in order to fully meet the needs of the customer; issues like specifications, language, and electrical requirements all need to be resolved. In a non-networked environment, the process can take some months to complete, due to the difficulty of accessing the information within the different locations and divisions of a multinational firm like Atlas Copco and the potential number of iterations with customers to make changes to a basic design.

Using a sales configuration tool operated by skilled sales technicians, Atlas Copco can create the right combination of products that meet exacting technical standards of engineering and heavy construction firms the world over.

Matching products to the needs of customers is not the only benefit of sales automation systems in a build-to-order business. Another key benefit of the configuration tool is shortening customers' decision cycles in that it reduces the time it takes to close the deal and the time to actually receive revenue. In addition, the extensive online product catalog helps Atlas Copco be able to ensure that salespeople can access information customized to customer/market needs (languages, units of measure); this will drive down the number of customer service calls. Finally, by ensuring the accuracy of the data and the validity of the products, Atlas Copco can prevent costly errors in product configuration.

Key Principles for Synchronizing Supply and Demand

Use pricing and personalization technologies to smooth demand volatility. This tactic draws on some of the key customer interaction and positioning capabilities outlined in the previous chapter. Effective personalization requires both technology and the organizational skill to make it meaningful. That often means a company must be able to identify the customers that respond to price changes or unique bundles in order to influence that demand and ultimately smooth their demand-supply relationshipsInformation standards make the data flow more effectively

Industry organizations like the Collaborative Planning, Fulfillment and Replenishment (CPFR) initiative are not only about what to collaborate on, they are also about how to collaborate. That is, standardizing data to enable demand data and supply data to work together effectively can only improve the reliability of both sets of concerns. With information standards and planning approaches shared within the industry synchronizing demand and supply because a routine matter.

Synchronization occurs through both management and technology. Creating effective supply response to direct and indirect demand requires a heavy emphasis on the planning and process perspective as well as the technology and information systems to provide the linkage. Some of the key strategies for enabling synchronization are created by relationship, supply partnerships and other ecosystem initiatives that create opportunity for both supplier, partner and ultimate customer.

Notes

1. Don Tapscott, David Ticoll, and Alex Lowy, *Digital Capital: Harnessing the Power of Business Webs* (Boston: Harvard Business School Press, 2000).
2. Bill Lakenan, Darren Boyd, and Ed Frey, "Why Cisco Fell: Outsourcing and Its Perils," *strategy+business*, Issue 24 (Third Quarter, 2001).
3. Lawrence M. Fisher, "From Vertical to Virtual: How Nortel's Supplier Alliances Extend the Enterprise," *strategy+business*, Issue 22 (First Quarter, 2001).
4. Industry Directions, *The Next Wave of Supply Chain Advantage: Collaborative Planning, Forecasting and Replenishment*, CPFR Survey Findings and Analysis, April 2000.
5. David Bovet and Joseph Martha, "Biogen Unchained," *Harvard Business Review*, May/June 2000, p. 28.

Part 2

Customer Ecosystem Case Studies

P art Two provides in-depth case studies of companies that are currently on the path of evolving a customer ecosystem. They have implemented technological tools in association with Pivotal Corporation and have changed the way they do business in many cases to enable new kinds of relationships with their customers and partners, changed the way that they organize their business in order to be successful in a network business environment.

- ◆ Intrawest, a leading ski and vacation property company.
- ◆ RBC Capital Markets, the technology market arm of investment bank RBC Dain Rauscher
- ◆ US Filter, an industrial water filtration manufacturer and system integrator
- ◆ Novozymes, Denmark-based, world leader in commercial and industrial enzymes

These case studies illustrate the 6 steps to creating a customer ecosystem. In particular, they illustrate key concerns relating to technology, strategy and customer experience.

The smart use of technology is dependent on aligning capabilities, adaptive strategies and the dynamics of the ecosystem. Some companies just get it right from the start,. They understand the change in mindset that is required to build effective linkages between the customer , an organization's capabilities and its technology.

Some of the questions we investigate in the case studies in Part II are discussed below.

Ecosystem Dynamics and Customer Experience

Complex customer ecosystems require companies constantly understand the flow of connection, influence, advocacy and. To assess alignment, companies need to investigate:

- How much involvement do customers expect or are capable of providing the customer relationships? Do we have the right connections for
- What linkages are necessary with partners and allies to create a broad network of demand?

Adaptive Strategies

Assessing the fit of adaptive strategies for thriving in a customer ecosystem:

- What is the emphasis for this ecosystem: demand creation or demand responsiveness?
- What kind of customer do we deal with primarily? Is there a range of customers with different levels of
- Is the strategy simple and robust enough to provide direction but still enable us to address new opportunities?

Customer Capabilities

Capabilities, by definition, are built from a linkage of organizational competencies and technology -enabled activity. The smart use of technology is dependent on two key components:

- Do we have the key competencies in place that support adaptive strategies and the needs of the ecosystem? Of critical concern is understanding and adapting ot the ecosystem:
  - Do we have adequate demand sensing (understanding) capabilities in place to ensure learning and facilitate the sharing of knowledge through out the organization?
  - Are we able to put our best minds into engineering our business for the purpose of adapting to market, technology and organizational changes?
- Does the organizational and technical infrastructure support potential change in future market?
- Does the information systems ensure integration with the customers and partners through processes and activities?

8

Managing Demand
at Intrawest

M atthew Dunn has one of the most enviable office views in the world. From his office at Whistler/Blackcomb mountain just two hours north of Vancouver, British Columbia, he has a stunning vista of the Coastal Range of mountains. In front of him, the quaint Whistler Village spreads out like a fairy tale village from Hans Christian Andersen.

As the CIO of Intrawest Corporation, Dunn may has a challenging job. Tasked with knitting together 16 premier ski properties across North America and Europe, he is required to create a consistent technology face for a business whose character is driven by unyielding physical assets and often eccentric hospitality industry personalities.

Another critical challenge is to create an effective virtual presence for a vacation company with a very physical value proposition—vacationing outdoors.

Market Environment

After nearly two decades of growth driven by the baby boomers, the ski business slowed in the 1990s. Aging boomers began to trade in their skis for golf clubs and younger generations failed to pick up the slack. The trend has not reversed itself in recent years. If anything, the situation has gotten worse. According to a recent report, the number of downhill skiers in the United States dipped last year to a 10-year low—7.4 million, down 30% from 1994.[1]

This slowdown has led a shakeout in the ski resort business. Strapped for customers and cash, a number of ski hills have closed. Those remaining have gone or are going to one of two approaches: the small hill catering to a large number of locals or the amenity-filled mega resort.

The latter approach is well suited to re-attracting the baby boomer generation. With plenty of disposable income, these individuals are seeking not just a ski trip, but an overall resort *experience*. For the resort owner, the challenge is not just in creating first-class skiing, but also in providing enough non-skiing activities to keep visitors for several ways. Only by obtaining a far higher return on investment per customer can the owner justify the tremendous capital investment necessary to develop the resort facilities.

Customer Experience

Reducing hassles for skiers is possibly the most important ingredient, not only to individual ski operations, but also to the industry as a whole.

As a novice skier, you must put up with the entire hassle of booking accommodations, then lining up for lift tickets, then lining up for equipment rental, then lining up for the lifts. Not a desirable undertaking.

Intrawest Corporation has tried to create a customer experience that not only is free of hassle, but incorporates critical aspects that complement the personality of the people who come to the ski resort. Kinetic, animated, and active: these are the three main adjectives that describe the ski vacationer. Not content with a resort experience that is passive, Intrawest's customer wants a clear path to the action.

Skiing is not just a vacation; for many it is a vocation—a calling. The skier lifestyle is one of heavy involvement. For avid skiers, this means challenging themselves to conquer more difficult runs or more difficult mountains. Customers like to be able to experience other locations, but also over time like to be able to remain loyal to the superior experience offered by some facilities.

It also may mean investing in the lifestyle of a ski center, by owning vacation property, in order to ensure that they are part of the action and that they avoid the complications of hotel and resort bookings. It may also be because ownership reduces the hassle of packing all the gear that is necessary for a complete ski experience.

Among the first challenges for Intrawest to create the ultimate experience for its customers is to get the connections right. The mechanics of the hospitality and

Relationship Risk and Investment	Shared entertainment, common bond to the ski and boarding lifestyle.
	Customers invest in the lifestyle and real estate.
Knowledge Capital and Shared Development	Ability to create a tailored unique combination of options for ski vacation.
Advocacy	High potential for customer to influence others on the supplier's behalf.
Information Flow and Connection	Services and activities appear integrated, a sense of winter sports community.
	Customers provide information on vacation plans, preferences, and other requirements.
Overall Customer Activism	Traditionally, customers have been more passive. Intrawest is definitely moving them toward a more collaborative role, with the influence of co-development technology.

Table 8-1. Intrawest relationship with customers

lodging organization are quite different from the mountain operations organization. As the Intrawest people work hard to make these connections, their ability to surround the customers appropriately with the amenities, services, and experience they desire improves incrementally. "One of the challenging parts about our operation," Dunn states, "is that we have multiple, non-integrated businesses ... ski hill, restaurants, lodging, gift shops, real estate. We're working towards tying together our systems in an integrated, seamless fashion. Easier said than done, though."

Intrawest: The Mega-Resort Company

Intrawest Corporation pioneered and perfected this mega-resort strategy. After beginning as a residential and office real estate company in the mid-1970s, the Vancouver-based organization made a key strategic move in 1986. That year, it acquired the struggling Blackcomb ski resort some 90 minutes north of the city, part of CEO Joe Houssian's plan to cash in on what he calls "the last great real estate boom of this century—recreational real estate."[2]

In the early 1990s, the company went public on the Toronto Stock Exchange and proceeded to acquire a number of other ski resorts. In 1994, it divested its urban real estate arm and shifted management focus entirely to four-season mountain resorts.

More focused than ever, the company embarked on an aggressive growth strategy, acquiring seven major ski hills in five years and also diversifying into non-ski resorts. Intrawest Corporation is now the leading developer and operator of village-centered destination resorts across North America. It owns 10 mountain resorts, including Whistler/Blackcomb, North America's most popular mountain resort. In addition, the company owns one warm-weather resort, 18 golf courses, and a premier vacation ownership business, Club Intrawest. In 1999-2000, the Intrawest network of resorts had 6.2 million skier visits and 546,000 rounds of golf.

Performance Measures

The company's aggressive growth has translated into strong financial performance. Between 1996 and 2000, for example, company revenues increased from $208 million to $815 million.[4] Income from continuing operations also increased by nearly 400%, jumping from $14 to $52 million.

By most common standards, these are the measures that count. But to a company that professes to "build its business around its customers, not its mountains," these measures are simply not the only measures of interest. Traditional asset-based accounting does not provide quite enough perspective on how well the company strategy is working. Additional information on the customer, including satisfaction and loyalty, the organization, and the effectiveness of the technology deployment, is top-of-mind for Houssian and Dunn. "We need to broaden our measures" from Dunn's perspective. "A customer asset is not just a name on a mailing list."

The Right Attitude

Employment at an Intrawest resort like Whistler/Blackcomb swells from under 2000 in mid-summer to over 4500 at the height of ski season. In the ski business, most seasonal employees are given a brief introduction to their new jobs and sent on their way.

In order to achieve the customer experience that it is striving for, Intrawest makes a two-week training investment in seasonal employees, who may never come back. The training, coupled with extensive pre-screening for hiring practices, ensures that the seasonal employee is equipped with the right attitude and the right information on company policy to give the right impression to guests.

In addition, the company uses simple manual processes like a "playbook" that provides employees information on the right way to handle customers in whatever situation they might encounter.

From a technology perspective, Intrawest has chosen applications for managing customers that are easily understood with little training. As Dunn says, they have chosen applications that "a college kid who's there for the winter will be able to pick up and use and be a part of the team."

Waves of Change

Not unlike a collection of Intrawest mountain properties, the jagged pattern of demographic groups participating in ski or snowboard activity is quite striking. The highest peak would coincide with skiers hitting the age of 18. The next peak—although much lower—would occur about eight to 10 years later, as the young professional skier returns to the slopes. A still smaller peak occurs about another 10 years later, as those dedicated skiers brave enough to bring their families return. The final bunny hill appears as the active empty nesters return.

But, an interesting dilemma emerges as the question of customer behavior and market potentialities is compared with revenue streams. To build a higher-margin, sustainable business, the biggest challenge for Intrawest is to build the demand management to improve the ultimate revenue opportunity across the board. In terms of total revenue value from ancillary activities from each phalanx of skiers, the older groups nearly match the youngest skiers despite being outnumbered greatly. Of course, this is because the older skier can afford the higher-value rooms, restaurant meals, and other services. A traditional CRM marketing approach would focus in on the higher-value customers, in this case the older, wealthier skier. But this would no doubt result in long-term failure for Intrawest and the winter sports industry, because it would not be building a secure base.

So the short answer for long-term success is really a question of getting more kids to the ski hills. Through the process of listening to customers by conducting extensive research, Intrawest introduced the Parent Pass last year. This allows parents to share a season pass, so each week either parent can take the kids to the ski hill as the other parent does other things. A very successful new product in its own right, of course, the pass has an added benefit in that the kids may get to the hill more often and in greater numbers. In a way, this builds the base of future revenue.

The avid skier has a different set of issues. The hassle of lining up for tickets and stuff will just annoy him or her. "People don't go to a ski hill to stand in line," notes Vice President of Marketing Michael Cobb.

It seems obvious that marketing and customer management staff also consider skiing and winter sports as a vocation. With this insider track, they are able to model the process that they would like to experience in order to ensure that the online experience closely approximates the ultimate experience. Regular visits to ski resorts in Europe help keep the Intrawest team fresh with ideas—a research gig no one would turn down.

Distributed Capabilities

The complexity of information systems at an Intrawest resort is considerable because of the disparate businesses necessary to enable the "human animation" business. At each location there are the systems necessary for point of sale at numerous sites: ski rental, lessons, accommodations, restaurants, and gift shops, to name a few. The driver of these systems obviously was to resolve the transaction problems. With each new offering to improve the experience, the company risks increasing the hassle at each new stop.

Understanding

Experience with customer relationship management software has led people like Dunn to question the ability of most applications to create meaningful knowledge of customers. "The CRM experience has always struck me as somewhat manipulative and superficial," says Dunn. It is this kind of pressure to be above and beyond the ordinary that pushes others to dig a little deeper.

Intrawest, like many others, has undertaken data-mining exercises, albeit on a more limited basis. One such exercise identified a customer of the Stratton, Vermont location who ranked very near the top in terms of expenditure but did not actually participate in any mountain activities.

So far, Intrawest's ability to create and disseminate customer knowledge has not been process-oriented. Learning and inquiry are periodic. But it is coming. What patterns are they looking for in the instances where customers create their own experience?

Personalization: Vacation Planner

To counter the hassles of the core group of customers, the avid skiers, Intrawest conceived the vacation planner. This is a flexible configuration tool that enables users to create a total package of accommodations, travel arrangements, ski rental, and the like as necessary for a hassle-free vacation at any of 16 Intrawest ski resorts. In many respects, this tool is like the puppet master, pulling strings with the other systems in order to get the appropriate responses. Customers using the vacation planner receive their lift tickets at check-in and, hopefully, will be welcomed by name.

Engagement Capabilities

Steadily the real estate sales business is becoming automated using Pivotal Relationship software. As an integrated marketing and sales organization, the resort condominiums sales operation is making progress on improved targeting

Servicing Capabilities

Disparate businesses unfortunately lead to different systems for managing the customer. In the hotel segment, the business has made some progress toward creating a seamless experience.

One of the less traditional benefits of customer relationship management software is the apparent time savings from productivity improvements that are enabled through automation. At Intrawest this is viewed differently. It's much more a function of enabling the customer care employees to do their jobs, rather than deal with technicalities. From Cobb's perspective, "the information system empowers the employee. With all the arrangements taken care of, the employee can focus on helping to create the best experience. Staff members can address guests by name and help them out, instead of being gatekeepers. Employees don't want to be the 'bad guys,' making visitors wait half an hour for their ski rentals."

The intention of the customer service process is to increase customer satisfaction in such a way that the satisfaction translates into repeat bookings (loyalty)—and culminates in a visitor's decision to purchase property at one of Intrawest's resorts.[5]

Deconstructing the service capability at Intrawest: it is composed of an organizational competency relating to the desired entertainment image coupled with technology that frees up time to concentrate on the entertainment aspect of the business.

Intrawest: Managing Demand

Intrawest has recognized that market demand is built through a series of dependencies:

- Declining participation in skiing and snowboarding has been identified. The market is heavily competitive, due to maturation and consolidation.
- The dominant customer roles are clear: avid skiers are activist, taking a strong role to get what they want; wealthier skiers may be collaborators, providing an exchange of information for ownership.
- Critical partners in the demand management are the tour operator and the product suppliers.

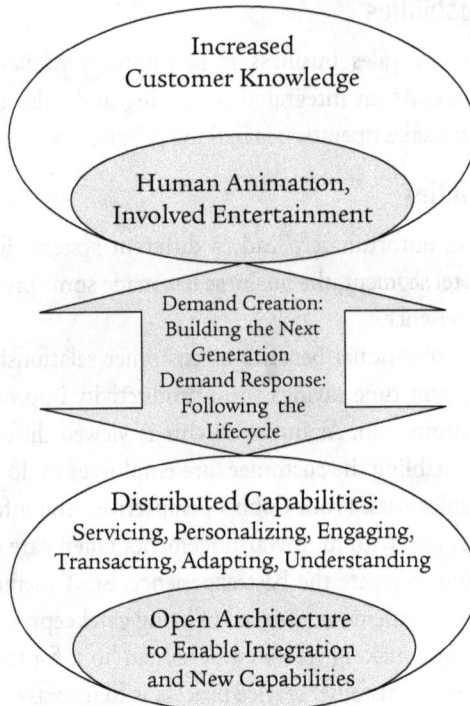

Figure 8-1. Intrawest strategic capabilities

Adaptive Strategies

Striving to create demand in the active vacation (particularly winter sports) market, Intrawest is attempting to be the leader just as Disney is the leader in the amusement vacation market.

Intrawest leverages ecosystem resources primarily by owning the supporting parts of the ecosystem, due to its desire to closely control the customer experience in the vacation villages.

Enabling younger skiers to participate in the sport creates long-term demand. At the same time, Intrawest responds to traditional sources of demand by ensuring access and quality of service.

The primary objectives for integrating with Intrawest's customer information systems are collaboration and reconfiguration. This is due to the strong role of the customer in creating value and Intrawest's interest in building long-term demand. Intrawest would like to reconfigure the network somewhat, to regain a balance of power with the customer in order to ensure the lifecycle of demand. Typical partners and intermediaries in the active winter sports vacation demand management will primarily be concerned about responding to demand rather than creating demand.

Information Technology

Open architecture is being developed to enable additional participants into the customer ecosystem. Other participants, like tour operators and even the companies that are owned by Intrawest but not integrated, will be enabled eventually to participate in customer information.

From an organizational perspective, Intrawest has excellent linkage of employee culture and the desired culture for customers that highly reflect the company's "reason for being."

Distributed Capabilities

Intrawest has deployed capabilities that enable a seamless, frictionless customer experience. It has focused on some key barriers to satisfaction and repeat visits to create more loyal customers. The chart below (Figure 8-2) summarizes how it has built capabilities for customer experience.

Distributed Capabilities	Capability = Competency + Technology – Enabled Activity
Positioning Capabilities	Engage—Real estate migration strategy and competency + sales application
	Adapt—Willingness to work with customer directly + technology to meet individuated needs
	Understand—appropriate understanding of demographic patterns (mental models) + data-mining capabilities
	Influence—Long-term perspective and promotional offers + online and offline customer applications
Interaction Capabilities	Fulfill—seamless delivery of purchases + automated activities for issuing tickets and scheduling activities to complete fulfillment
	Service—extensive training (service playbook) + service applications that enable more focus on customer
	Transact—broad perspective of transaction needs + increased integration of transaction functionality
	Personalize—profiling and strategy for individual behavior + online technology for personalization and integration of personal preference information

Figure 8-2. Intrawest capabilities for customer experience

Value in the Ecosystem

For Intrawest and many other companies, adaptation to demand conditions will be the acid test for their capabilities. From a straight financial perspective, the return for Intrawest from extending capabilities to customers has paid back the investment in about one full winter season. Specifically, the value of technology investment has been from increased sales throughout the network and a higher level of participation by both skiers and snowboarders at all of its locations. Generating *network-effect* return will be possible by continually adapting and influencing change in its "human animation" business. This is the next stage of its customer ecosystem.

Notes

1. Alex Markels, "Selling the Snowplow," *Newsweek*, 137(3) (January 15, 2001), p. 57.
2. William C. Symonds, "The Club Med of the Ski Slopes?," *Business Week*, March 18, 1996, p. 64.
3. Felicity Long, "Diversity Spurs Firm's Success," *Travel Weekly*, 59(78) (September 28, 2000), p. 25.
4. www.intrawest.com/about/investor/financial_reports.html. All figures in US dollars.
5. www.pivotal.com/customers/cs_intrawest.htm.
6. www.intrawest.com/about/overview/ourmission.html.

9

Ecosystem Strategy at RBC Capital Markets

O n his way to another appointment in the Boston area, Marc Saunders,[1] one of the top specialists in the biotech team at Wall Street investment banking house RBC Capital Markets, receives a brief, pointed communiqué on his BlackBerry wireless device to call an institutional investor that he has been trying to influence for weeks. The information he's received is about a key announcement made by a company RBC Capital Markets represents and, along with the solid research his team has provided to the portfolio manager, it enables him to persuade his target that the time is right for a key trade. The call delivers the right leverage and a large block trade swings the way Saunders had been hoping, all in less than 20 minutes.

Complexity

The financial services industry is moving through an incredibly dynamic period in its history, with government deregulation, market volatility, and a heightened interest in stock market investment prompting huge and ongoing changes.

Volatility and complexity typify the overall environment. Never in history have so many people participated in the stock market. Never in history has so much information been available to evaluate investment opportunities.

In this context of information acceleration, there may be only two ways to compete: brawn and brains. Brawn, in the form of massive capital access, is the basic approach of a J.P. Morgan Chase or a Goldman Sachs. Information provided by companies with capital power has a way of getting noticed. As for the smaller investment house, relevance and focus can help, but not guarantee, its effort to cut through the barrage of information targeted at portfolio managers in the pension and mutual fund houses. Brains, in the form of corporate learning to provide appropriate context for individual decision makers, are the only alternative for the boutique investment firms competing for attention in a crowded and chaotic investment environment.

The Transaction Triangle

Institutional investment decisions are not arbitrary or impulsive. Decisions are made when the fullness of research and the interpretation enabled by experience collide with events that necessitate a critical transaction. Working together on this decision is the "transaction triangle" that each and every institutional investor—be it a pension fund, a mutual fund, or other large investor—puts to the task of what comes down to a simple transaction. This powerful triumvirate consists of a portfolio manager, a research analyst, and a trading desk.

Portfolio managers have overall responsibility for a fund or group of funds and their job, of course, is to maximize performance. Mutual fund customers know that each portfolio manager has a style and a set of principles. In concert with the rest of the team, the manager makes critical decisions on behalf of thousands or millions of people. While the portfolio manager directs the research activity, the research analysts are often the unseen forces that drive large trading blocks. The trading desk also can influence the decision, when critical conditions are apparent in the market and if the desk is closely attuned to the needs of the portfolio manager. Influencing capability targeted at the transaction triangle is critical to driving demand and creating the right experience for RBC Capital Markets customers.

Creating a unique customer experience is not easy, in the competitive investment banking sector. Each institutional investor has a clear focus that's promoted through the literature. "There's all kinds of research on Wall Street. The problem is that 90% of it's garbage and only 10% is good, fundamental research," says Ted Mortonson, head of RBC Capital Markets' Institutional Sales and Trading Groups. Institutional investors receive a huge amount of investment promotion material—and much of it is not necessarily relevant to the investment interests of their particular institution. Turning information into insight is often all about timing.

Relationship Risk and Investment	Quality research, information delivered in context.
Knowledge Capital and Shared Development	Few new products are developed jointly, primarily created by the supplier. Opportunities for new business, however, may be jointly developed on an ad hoc basis.
Advocacy	Critical concern is the potential for advocacy and influence, as institutional investors have a great deal of influence if they want to use it.
Information Flow and Connection	Investment in connection is primarily one way, from DRW to its clients.
Overall Customer Activism	Customers are demanding and active in getting their demands, but are increasingly collaborative.

Table 7-1. Characteristics of RBC Capital Markets in relation to customer

Business Strategy

RBC Capital Markets is the equity capital markets division of RBC Dain Rauscher, active in investment banking and equity markets. The Capital Markets division focuses on five industry sectors: technology, energy, healthcare, financial services, and consumer services. It evolved out of a smaller investment bank, Dain Raucher Wessels, known for strengths in technology (the leading underwriter of network technology deals in 1999) and energy (the leading underwriter of energy deals in 1999). Primarily due to the acquisition in 1998 of Wessels, Arnold & Henderson, a privately held investment banking and institutional brokerage firm, RBC Capital Markets continues to as a focused leader in its five primary industry sectors. However, with only $60 billion in assets under management control, RBC Capital Markets ranks well back of leading investment bankers like J.P. Morgan Chase.

Leveraging Knowledge

For the RBC Capital Markets division to compete, it has to continue to focus and to leverage both its experience and its approach to gathering information. RBC Capital Markets believes it gets into the trenches on deals like no other.

A good example is its success with Juniper Networks (www.juniper.net), for which RBC Capital Markets was the primary underwriter. Research analysts evaluated the hardware and the software that ostensibly made Juniper Network's high-end network equipment and backbone routers for the Internet different. At the time, Cisco dominated the low-, mid-, and high-end router markets. And, of course, Cisco had significant name brand recognition at a time when a crowded market was giving few other "wannabes" the time of day.

Now, other investment houses do significant research, including corporate visits, technology reviews, and the like. Many of the other shops believe that superior research is enough reason for the institutional investors to pay attention to their message.

RBC Capital Markets takes it further. First, research is disseminated through an internal knowledge management system. Second, this research is linked to the CRM system to ensure that the right information gets to the potential customers that might actually listen.

The Juniper Networks deal was a success. According to Mortonson, "They reached 35% of the high-end router market. How did we help them do it? A lot of it had to do with educating Wall Street on the technology itself, showing them how Juniper excelled and where Cisco was deficient."

Extending Capabilities

The second key to success for RBC Capital Markets is to make the connection between the right research and the right customer. According to Mike Thibault, the company's manager of applications services for the capital markets trading area, one of the biggest challenges following the acquisition of Wessels was to improve and customize services for the combined institutional customer base. This meant making better use of all the information it held about its customers.

Faced with a variety of customer databases that were limited in functionality as well as being independent islands of data, Thibault set about creating a common customer database. "We used to have many different contact databases that we would work off," he recalls. "With the environment as it is today in the brokerage business, we must have integrated solutions that allow everyone to access the same information from anywhere, anytime. Within the financial services industry, our customers require us to provide more timely information that is focused toward their needs."

Thibault says customers have made it clear that they do not want generic "stock picks" from brokers; they want very specific recommendations based on their known needs and preferences. "They want to have calls that are focused on what they need. With the databases we used to use, we couldn't derive that information. This problem was a big stumbling block which prevented our institutional salespeople from focusing on our customers and on providing more effective solutions and products."

In order to do this, however, RBC Capital Markets forced participation from leading traders, salespeople, and analysts to come up with the business rules that will ensure that the right approaches and the right messages are being put forward at the right time. As an investment, albeit a soft-dollar one, the input cost of time and money has been significant—not to mention unheard of in the brokerage industry. Taking top earners off the line for 10% of their day to help map out the business processes that will make other salespeople effective is challenging and raises the expectations of all traders for increased success.

Critical inputs for the business rules are investment strategies of specific institutional investors in conjunction with investment histories. From this information, highly developed data queries enable RBC Capital Markets to provide proprietary research that is tightly targeted to each institutional investor.

The payoff is delivering customers not just more content but also the relevant context. "To give you some indication, before we had these linkages, we had only about a 30% rate. Now we've gotten our percentage of getting the trade up to 60% or 70%. That's a big difference," says Mortonson. As RBC Capital Markets has discovered, effective creation of engagement capabilities is about ensuring relevance.

Furthermore, it has cut the cost of doing business with its institutional investors by a material amount. The company estimates that it has saved 25%-30% on mailing costs alone over the past year by simply sending customers the information they want, rather than using a "scattergun" approach to overload them with too much information.

Raising the Bar

Another difference that RBC Capital Markets' customer process and business architecture make to the customer is speed of response. Not only are outbound, persuasive contacts more targeted and effective, response to questions or issues is much quicker. If a customer calls to talk to a salesperson or an analyst and the person is not immediately available, a message is sent to his or her wireless BlackBerry pager. Depending on the person's status within the RBC Capital Markets system, the call can be sent top priority and returned within minutes.

As noted by Mortonson, "Historically, Wall Street takes days to call back. Sometimes, the call is never returned. With our current system, though, we can alert sales reps and can return the call in five or 10 minutes. If we can do that consistently, that does a lot for our reputation on Wall Street." RBC Capital Markets is able to do this because of business rules. If the analyst is not logged in at his or her desk, then the communication immediately goes to the BlackBerry device. Strict adherence to business rules is required or the salesperson or analyst can actually lose money.

RBC Capital Markets customers notice a distinct difference in service. Independent customer satisfaction research indicates that institutional investors recognize that the timeliness and quality of information and service rank among the highest, even compared with much larger investment houses.

Organizational Culture

There is a certain intensity attached to any Wall Street firm. RBC Capital Markets is no exception. But you get the feeling that there really is more teamwork than in the average shop, much of it resulting from a number of core processes and their linkage to the critical element of compensation.

In order to design the relationship management system, RBC Capital Markets invested its top money earners' time into the creation of "business rules." As much as 10% of their time was spent on identifying and recording the best approaches they knew and practices to create their own success. "We had the top person from each area outline their business rules on a whiteboard," says Mortonson. In his opinion, most CRM implementations fall short because they adopt the standard business rules of the software vendor or the integrator. Furthermore, Mortonson strongly suggests that business process for customer management cannot be standardized and is really the most important source of differentiation a company can have.

Frequently, companies get pushback from top salespeople when they attempt to tap into corporate business rules as RBC Capital Markets has for its CRM system. There is a common perception that sharing their best practices will in some way detract from their earning power. RBC Capital Markets has both direct and indirect tactics to persuade the top earners to share and to stick around while the rest of the team ramps up.

"When you get down to it, compensation is what really costs us money. There's not much in the way of overhead—you give them a PC, a phone, what does that cost? It's compensation that adds up. If you can do more with the same number of people, it makes a huge difference." According to Mortonson, the efficiency gain from process sharing enables even the top earners to become more efficient and thus gain more revenue. Wall Street companies trying to grow their business in the past have usually added more staff and played a "numbers game" of "more calls multiplied by current hit rate equals more sales."

Better efficiency in managing the customer processes also helps as a retention tool at RBC Capital Markets. Mortonson believes that "Wall Street is 100% intellectual capital and relationships. If you can prevent turnover, you preserve those relationships" and those relationships turn into earning power for both the employee and the company.

Application Infrastructure

Three critical application suites enable RBC Capital Markets to operate its business: research and knowledge management, transaction processing and financial systems, and customer management systems. Conceptually, the three application suites are aligned through the most important common denominator: the customer record. The customer management system enables the knowledge management system to provide information in context to people who care, ultimately yielding a transaction that drives the financial systems but is also is recorded in the customer database. Further honing of the customer profile is enabled through analysis of historical transaction data.

In order to create an effective infrastructure aligned with the customer ecosystem, RBC Capital Markets has had some growing pains. Its first attempt at CRM was using traditional client-server technology. The current system is Web-based. "It builds upon the internal functionality of the organization and will be the brains of our next generation XML-based Web site."

This architecture is also critical to the linkage to RBC Capital Markets' wireless network. The open architecture approach enables wireless linkages by more than just e-mail; it can be fully integrated with the business rules that drive revenue generation for RBC Capital Markets.

The creation of a customer ecosystem is being conducted in two phases. The first phase is really a CRM implementation, focusing on the internal systems and processes. In Mortonson's eyes, "Its success all depends on getting the business rules right."

"By discovering and embedding all the underlying business rules," says Mortonson, "we were able to create a system in which all the necessary data is only one screen away. What we have created is a database of tremendous value—essentially a knowledge base of where Wall Street is going."

Demand Driven Strategy: Assessing the Fit at RBC Capital Markets

Most strategy is simple to conceive and difficult to execute. In the case of RBC Capital Markets, the ecosystem it is creating is simple and very balanced. The diagram below (Figure 9-1) shows that the needs of the business environment, particularly the customers, are insight, immediacy, and leverage. The business strategy is simple: a focused strategy that depends on gaining synergy between knowledge and relationship, with the intent to continue to accelerate the standard that the firm sets relative to competitors. And finally, the business architecture provides the ability to deliver context and relationship in a real-time setting.

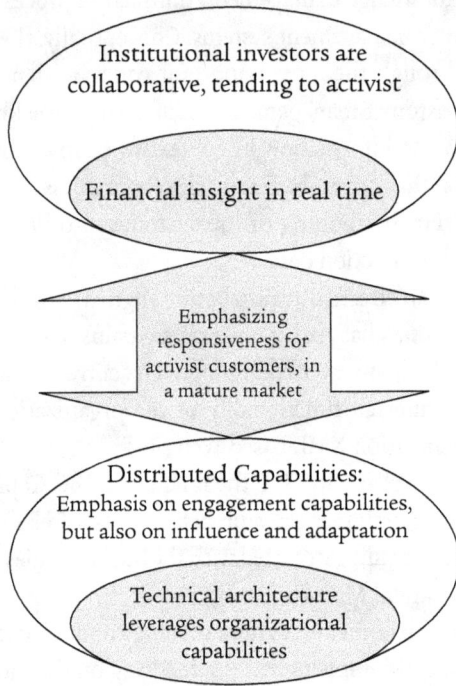

Figure 9-1. RBC Capital Markets: In real time

Ecosystem Dynamics

The ecosystem dynamics for RBC Capital Markets are fast and intense, regardless of whether the market is on an upturn or a downswing. The need for rapid response and rapid action is intensifying.

Institutional customer relationships are demanding and, while not fickle, they can be fleeting if performance of the investment bank is inconsistent or unreliable. Relationships can last if maintained according to the needs of the institutional investor.

Customers demand a collaborative relationship in determining what information is valuable, but with the level of competition in investment banking, institutional investors are definitely a powerful audience.

Adaptive Strategies

The overall business context is to participate in the broad network of investment banking as a differentiated competitor. The key source of differentiation is the firm's ability to process and target information to specific customers.

Key resources for RBC Capital Markets are the human elements that create relationships and that develop analysis for customers. These resources are extended to customers through traditional channels as well as through Internet technology.

Capability Fit

RBC Capital Markets has applied key staff to the creation of capabilities for positioning its organization relative to competitors. Extending these capabilities out to customers is a critical competitive element.

Figure 9-2 shows the key capabilities leveraged by RBC Capital Markets in the customer ecosystem.

Information Technology

Current technical architecture enables future change of the business applications and in the organizational capabilities.

Organizationally, the company has accepted that the cost of not involving the best people in creating the right technology and business capability exceeds the opportunity cost of taking key producers away from their usual work. This marks RBC Capital Markets as a company that will enable the right people to tackle an organizational need for change as markets or conditions change.

Teamwork also exists in an organization whose peers typically do not enjoy the benefit of teamwork. Compensation and culture are critical tools that RBC Capital Markets uses to reinforce this climate of collaboration.

Business Impact

Even though strategic fit is important, so is ROI. With this tight integration of environment, strategy, and architecture, the information system yielded payback

117

Distributed Capabilities	Capability = Competency + Technology-Enabled Activity
Positioning Capabilities	Engage—RBC Capital Markets has leveraged the top performers engagement capabilities, turning them in to "business rules" + enabled these activities through relationship management application
	Adapt—Organization focuses on rapid response to changing market conditions + enabled through "push" technology to ensure business activity
	Understand—In order to tailor positioning messages, the organization has listened to customers, information needs + enabled analysis and investment advice to be collected according to customer need
Interaction Capabilities	Service—Organization concentration on resolving customer issues + enabled to respond rapidly
	Transact—Transactions are completed through industry-standard trading systems.
	Personalize—Soon to implement personalization functionality online. Recognition on unique needs of investment participants, roles and the different focuses of institutional investors + customer profiling by increasingly granular characteristics

Figure 9-2. Key capabilities leveraged by RBC Capital Markets in the customer ecosystem

in "about two months," according to Mortonson. Being in contact with the right person, at the right time, with the right message has captured deals that they know did not come their way in the past. And once the system is under way, the cost per transaction is infinitesimal.

Where to from Here?

The next step is to connect with the customer more directly, through online capability. Complementing the real-world skills of the sales people and analysts, RBC Capital Markets plans to enable its customers to tell more about what they want to know. In addition to profiling through past transaction histories and salespersons' knowledge of the customers, an online customer interface will capture the customers' future interests and issues. For Mortonson, two adjectives describe this effort: *collaborative* and *personalized*. "Our eventual goal is to have the customers do more of the work for themselves."

Knowing that just as RBC Capital Markets wants to accelerate and raise the bar for customers, many competitors do the same. "The reality is that, going forward, data is only going to grow," Mortonson says. "There's a whole mushroom cloud effect, meaning that finding the needle in the haystack is only going to become harder." Creating a synergy among the sales rep, the research analyst, the trading floor, and the customers' counterparts in a real-time and online environment is the challenge to deliver on that strategy.

Note

1. The name of the individual is disguised for this profile. The actual event is factual.

10

USFilter: Organizing Around the Customer

As Norm Taylor[1] unlatched the gate of the chain-link fence around Ford Motor Company's new water treatment plant for the Tennessee SUV production facility, he was completely unaware of all the staff at USFilter who had participated in this project and would not see its ultimate conclusion. Since the company he previously worked for had been acquired in 1991, he had learned much more about the water treatment business than he expected to learn. His role as a water treatment product salesman was also so much more complex because of all the different people he had to interact with and the new sales process that he needed to learn. But it had been good for him, business was good, and his own salary was increasing, so he knew something was right about USFilter.

Based in Palm Desert, California, USFilter is a leading provider of outsourced water services, including the operation of water and wastewater treatment systems at customer sites. It is also actively involved in the development of privatization initiatives for municipal water treatment facilities in the United States and around the world. Vivendi is a worldwide leader in environmental services as well as a major player in Europe's communications industry.

Business Environment

One of the first things that strike you about the market for water treatment products, services, and solutions is the variation in buying processes for the same basic outcomes.

Consumers, becoming more active in environmental issues with each passing day, want more and more control over the quality of the water that they buy for their families. More information about the process and the products provides them with a greater assurance about the water products they choose.

Industrial companies may have a variety of purchasing approaches depending on the type of purchase. An installation for a new facility may require a long proposal process, while purchasing replacement parts may be simple and easy. The trend clearly is for industrial companies to outsource more and more of their non-core functions.

Municipalities may have a range of needs to address, none more important than the public accountability for fiscal restraint. This means that they are under increased pressure to reduce municipal costs, which typically means fewer employees in expert roles.

The Strategy

Given the changes in customer structure and buying process, USFilter has evolved a business of myriad parts to attempt to deliver a complete customer solution.

Founded in 1990, USFilter has grown from $16 million in revenues to 2001 sales in North America of $4.2 billion. The company has grown through acquisition primarily, with more than 250 companies being combined into the main USFilter entity. A company that is committed to growth, the first phase of its growth strategy, clearly apparent during its first five years of existence, USFilter focused on technology consolidation, buying up many smaller companies to ensure that key solutions could be assembled from a broad range of products and technologies that were otherwise disconnected in the marketplace.

Organizing for Responsiveness

USFilter has formed teams of water treatment specialists who understand the needs of specific industries. These market specialists are entrusted with the task of matching USFilter's capabilities with each customer's specific needs. Areas of specialization include automotive, biotech/pharmaceuticals, food and beverage,

121

hydrocarbon and chemical processing, medical research and laboratory, microelectronics, municipal, power, primary metals, pulp and paper, and residential and commercial.

These teams of specialists are composed of several key players who come together to serve a customer or a business opportunity: an industry market manager who acts as the quarterback for USFilter's approach to customers and opportunities, direct salespeople who represent USFilter in most industrial markets, independent manufacturer's representatives who maintain contact and relationships with municipal governments for USFilter and other companies, strategic account managers who build relationships with major manufacturers, the corporate projects group, which consists of specialists in engineering and architecture related to water treatment, and a team of project developers who may assemble financial and real estate development packages to create the ultimate in turnkey packages for the commercial, industrial, and municipal concerns.

The vision for this mode of organization has always been to rapidly respond to customer requests. But by being able to assemble skills and experience effectively, USFilter is better able than other companies to shape or form the way that its customers view the ultimate solution to their water treatment needs.

The second key element of USFilter's customer-oriented organization is the assemblage of disparate companies and technology into market groups. USFilter has positioned itself on the leading edge of water treatment technology, thereby offering its customers the broadest range of solutions for their particular water treatment needs. USFilter now owns or licenses more than 3,000 active patents worldwide and continues to develop technologies for the future at a rate of more than two patents per week. The company spends more than $50 million a year on research and development. Rather than focusing on selling new technologies to industrial or municipal buyers, the Industrial Products Group or the Water and Wastewater Group can solve problems in a way that happens to use more advanced technologies.

Connecting with the Customer

Municipalities and industrial corporations often no longer have the level of technical expertise to manage the water treatment process as they once did. Companies and governments alike have started to shed their non-core operations in favor of outsourcing. While this idea or tendency has begun to take hold, the process of making this decision is a long and arduous one. Decisions can take as long as 18 months for corporate and government organizations alike (see Table 10-1).

Relationship Risk and Investment	Contracted relationships, potential for risk sharing makes more commitment and mutual investment possible, but only in certain cases.
Knowledge Capital and Shared Development	Development of new products and solutions primarily driven by suppliers. Standards and requirements are set by organizations—not a two-way process.
Advocacy	A tight-knit community of municipalities can heavily influence opportunity for USFilter.
Information Flow and Connection	Generally, connection with industrial or municipal customers is limited to point issues. May be some input to product quality, safety, and cost-effectiveness.
Overall Customer Activism	Consumers becoming less passive. Municipalities are outsourcing and are thus less hands-on and more passive.

Table 10-1. USFilter relationships with customers

With a complex organization like USFilter that has been put together from many different businesses, each with their own traditions, the well-worn path of communications on customer issues has been one of e-mail, phone calls, and the informal "subterranean network" of contacts common to larger organizations.

Partner Leverage

Relationships with customers in the municipal sector and some industrial markets continue to be through manufacturers' representatives. These are commissioned agents who become part of the team when opportunity presents itself. Since they are the long-term associates of the customer, however, USFilter wants them to be more often a part of its team, as opposed to a part of its competitors.

Informal communications on complex issues within this environment were just not good enough for USFilter. A formal process for engagement underpinned by software was created to ensure that some simple but consistent rules are followed to connect with the customer.

For key customers and for specific opportunities, all of the appropriate team members are assigned to help in the process of creating solutions that bring forward the best in technology and service. USFilter has developed engagement capabilities by leveraging the competencies of the sales organization and creating technology-enabled activity in a customer relationship management system that captures relevant data about customers, but also automatically informs the team members that a new customer issue or new business opportunity has arisen. No longer do the jungle drums have to beat to ensure that the right people focus on the right opportunities.

Learning About Markets

Industry market managers have the responsibility to coordinate activities in their markets. From the information at their fingertips, they can learn about how USFilter has fared in specific opportunities. It is their job to learn why USFilter is winning or losing versus its competitors.

Because of the scale and scope of USFilter, its access to opportunities and thus to market information provides it with a substantial knowledge asset. Specialized market intelligence information providers like USABlueBook keep track of the ebb and flow of contract awards in industrial and municipal markets. USFilter, by tracking opportunities to a high level of granularity, has a counterpoint data set that enables it to verify or refute market trends that the rest of the market may wait weeks to identify and may not ever do so.

Companies utilizing CRM software often make the mistake of not creating process and accountability to turn the megabytes of data into information and ultimately into knowledge. USFilter holds the market manager accountable to learn about competitors and products and to participate with product development in new development and product modification.

One such example of learning about markets occurred in the power generation industry. A technical product offering, believed by USFilter to be competitive, was suffering consistent losses to another company. The power generation market manager, through analyzing simple win/loss rates in his market, identified the pattern. Several responses were planned, including pricing, solution combinations, and—in the medium term—changes to technical specifications.

Demand Management Infrastructure

Like many other companies, USFilter does not think of its infrastructure as enabling demand management. In its industry, however, customers' desire for controlling the interaction is limited. From an application infrastructure perspective, the appropriate level of connection is to maintain and evolve the existing channels.

An added benefit of USFilter's customer-oriented infrastructure is the ability to change and personalize with relative ease. Acquisitions and market changes are inevitable for USFilter. Committed to offering the best possible solutions under one roof for customers, it will add new products, technologies, and companies as the market demands. The application and processes for keeping the company focused on the customer must change as the market demands. "Many of companies that buy software and change their processes to match the software are making a mistake," says Moody. "We wanted to be able to change business processes flexibly without the long-term cost associated with changing our business."

Direct sales representatives currently manage communications with manufacturers' representatives. This will soon be augmented with Internet-based communications directly to customers.

While the company has had as many as 35 different legacy accounting and manufacturing systems that were not connected, investment decisions for implementation of information systems were obvious to USFilter. As they assembled the critical parts of a systems- and solutions-oriented business, the decision makers knew they would not be successful in maximizing their acquisition investments if they did not knit together a market-focused organization through their information systems strategy. "We would not have a solid business without solutions-oriented customers," notes Moody. "Without this kind of a customer relationship, the complexity of our products and technologies would be overwhelming." Not that integration of legacy systems is not important at USFilter; the transition of these systems will just take more time.

Employees and Culture

While flexibility over time is important for USFilter's customer process, there is fundamental structure and rhythm of work underlying how the company deals with customers. With over 600 employees connected, the customer relationship management approach remains the same for leads and opportunities and long-term account management. Customer teams may be composed of employees of several different predecessor companies and they have had to learn a new way of working. "The customer-engagement process and business system is helping our teams make the transition from product focus to market and customer focus," Moody points out. Over time he believes that new employees will not have any other tendency and the culture will become more consistent.

Although the strategy of solution orientation is commonplace and perhaps even somewhat passé, the secret to success is in implementation for USFilter.

125

"Execution is the key for us," says Moody. "We are a sales-oriented Old Economy company, trying to assemble the best solutions possible for our customer. It may not be too exciting, but it is essential for our success," he concludes.

Demand Driven Strategy: Assessing the Fit at USFilter

Business Environmental Fit

As we look specifically at the market for wastewater products and services, we can see that it is evolving in a different direction from many other markets. Rather than becoming more involved in the purchase process, manufacturing companies consider wastewater a secondary or tertiary concern and municipalities consider it a key, but specialized service. Since it is not central to the value proposition of companies, it is difficult to capture their attention for new technologies or product-oriented messaging. The primary concern of municipalities is providing services at the lowest possible cost.

In this business environment, the key players are fairly stable but with increasing demands:

◆ Industrial/municipal customers are seeking to outsource with specific performance standards. In a way, they are seeking less control over the function, but more control over the outcome.

◆ Distribution partners still provide access to customers and remain a key part of the business environment.

◆ Individual consumers are becoming more knowledgeable and thus more demanding.

Adaptive Strategies

USFilter has identified the market's need for solutions and responded by bringing 200-plus distinct companies together to create services and solutions. The company is trying to leverage its product resources for a market that is increasingly open to solutions.

Creating demand for water management solutions is the main thrust of its strategic approach. However, USFilter remains open to product sales through traditional distribution channels, thus continuing to be demand-responsive.

Technology Fit

USFilter has already identified that a key business architecture element required changing in order to match the strategy and the business environment. Specifically,

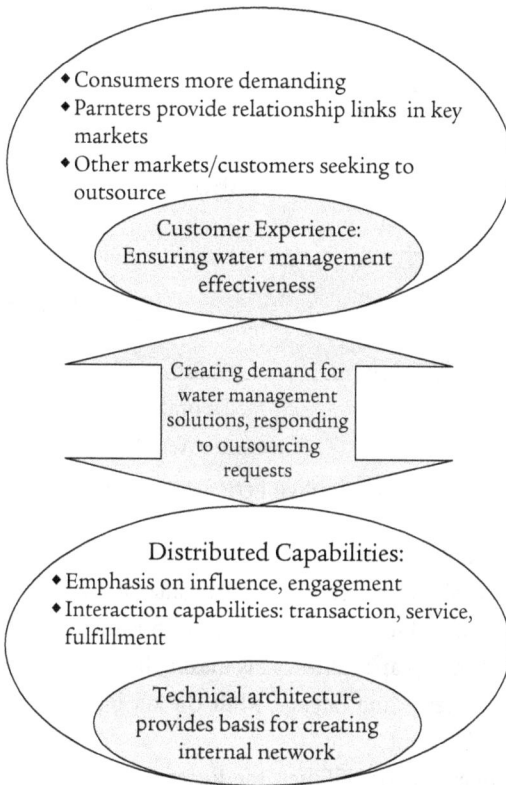

Figure 10-1. Assessing strategic fit at USFilter

the company needs to continue to change the culture from a product-centric, disconnected operating concept to a customer- and solution-centric approach.

One of the first steps of integrating the disparate companies that make up USFilter was to create a business architecture to enable an internal network to create more uniform customer-facing activities. The key task at USFilter is to build the information network and organizational climate that will enable further development of the business capabilities. It is this base architecture that future technology will need to connect.

Aligning Ecosystem Strategies

Unlike most of the other markets that we have examined, the market for wastewater treatment solutions is composed increasingly of customers that are passive customers, as defined in Chapter 2. According to the framework presented in Chapter 4, the appropriate approach to extending network capabilities would fall

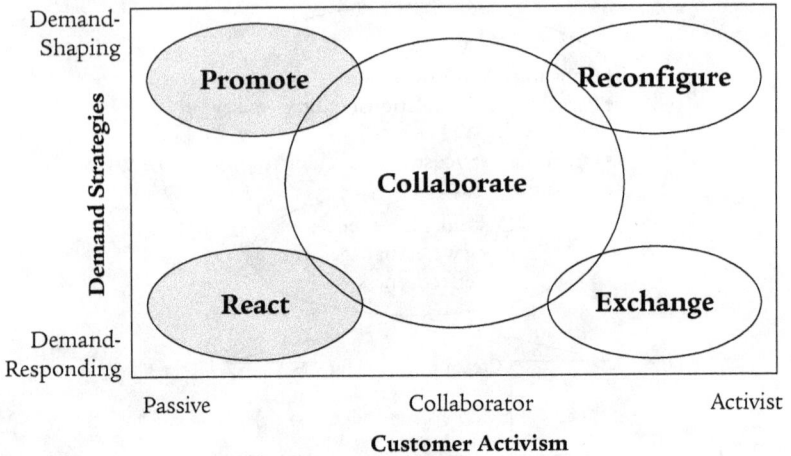

Figure 10-2. Framework for adaptive ecosystem strategies

into the Promote and React stances.

On the industrial/commercial/municipal side of USFilter's business, the Promote mode of demand management integration is therefore the recommended approach to extending capabilities. This means that the key positioning capabilities should be Influence and Engage, while the key interaction capabilities are Fulfill, Service, and Transact.

On the consumer side of USFilter, the React mode is most appropriate for integration with the value chain. This means that the key positioning capabilities will be Understand, Engage, and Adapt and the key interaction capabilities will be Fulfill, Service, Transact, and Personalize.

Where to from Here?

USFilter is a work in progress. New capabilities are being created to enable the desired customer experience and to fulfill the strategic focus on solutions. The capabilities distributed through both employees and partners of USFilter's Water and Wastewater Group are shown in Figure 10-3.

Note

1. Illustrative event only.

Distributed Capabilities	Capability = Competency + Technology-Enabled Activity
Positioning Capabilities	Engage—Solutions team orientation + systems to deploy team players for customer needs
	Influence—Creating solutions orientation in the marketplace + enabling activities of employees and partners through customer management system
Interaction Capabilities	Fulfill—Solutions-oriented fulfillment being developed further
	Service—Customer service responsiveness being developed
	Transact—Capabilities to complete solutions transactions being developed

Figure 10-3. USFilter capabilities

11

The Novozymes Ecosystem

"Uhen Novozymes launched the detergent enzyme Lipolase in 1988, we were the first company in the world to market an enzyme produced from genetically engineered microorganisms." This monumental achievement, prominently stated in Novozymes' 2001 Annual Report, has set the stage for both tremendous business success and heightened sensitivity within Novozymes on its role in society.

Since 1988 Novozymes has expanded the use of gene technology to become a versatile tool in discovering natural enzymes, generating artificial enzymes, and producing superior enzyme products. With its headquarters in Denmark and companies and offices in more than 25 countries, Novozymes sells enzymes in 130 countries and has more than 3,400 employees.

The Customer Experience

Like most companies, Novozymes' customers range from the very large, like multinational consumer products company Procter & Gamble, to the very small, like the Molinas Company of Sardinia, which supplies corks for wineries worldwide. In order to serve its customers' diverse range of needs, Novozymes has a diverse range of channels and tools for customers to interact with.

Relationship Risk and Investment	
Knowledge Capital and Shared Development	Potential for technical breakthrough, disruptive performance improvement.
Advocacy	
Information Flow and Connection	
Overall Customer Activism	

Table 11-1. Novozymes relationships with customers

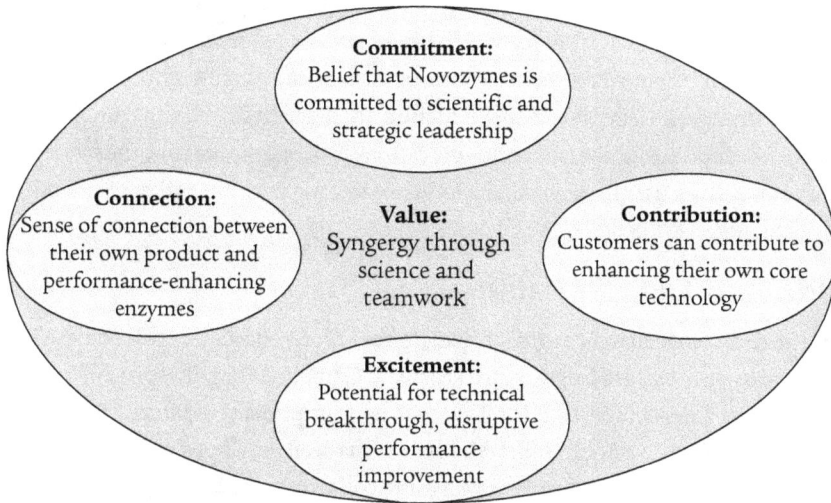

Figure 11-1. Novozymes' customer experience: sense of synergy

In order to enable effective, broad relationships with large organizations, like major breweries or distilleries, Novozymes may dedicate a specific major account team that deals with all of that customer's particular needs. Novozymes also works with distributors that build relationships with companies in specific industries and within certain geographies.

In about 1996, the organization, then called Novo Nordisk Enzymes, found that there was a broad range of practices for managing customers around the world. Operating in 20 countries worldwide, regional offices had different ways of dealing with customers depending upon which office served that particular company. With globalization, Novozymes found that customers were potentially experiencing variations in how they were being related to.

The customer experience can be as varied as the applications that Novozymes makes for its customers. Enzymes help a company to improve the quality or effectiveness of a product or process. In order for Novozymes to create targeted action for customers, it works closely with them or with industry researchers.

Adaptive Strategies

Novozymes has been researching into biotechnology since 1941 and, with very few exceptions, has been behind the launch of virtually all new industrial enzymes, from the lipases used to remove fatty stains from fabrics to the amylases used to manufacture sweeteners.

Research and development is a central part of Novozymes' strategy, exemplified by its commitment to allocate 11%-13% of revenues annually to research activities. Innovation, however, comes from both demand-creating and demand-following strategies. Heavy involvement in industry research as well as a combination of customer partnerships and communications processes round out the strategies that Novozymes uses to maintain its industry-leading position and dominant 45% market share.

Detergents: Customer Partnership

In the detergents market segment, Novozymes undertakes extensive co-development activities with leading partner Procter & Gamble (P&G). In April 2000, P&G announced a new innovation for Tide that uses proprietary Mannaway® enzyme technology to remove food stains. Mannaway has been developed by Novozymes in association with P&G as part of an ongoing collaboration. Mannaway represents a new group of enzymes called *mannanases*.

Novozymes works with many companies in the detergent industry. "If it is a major customer for us and if we are important for them, we can enter into an exclusive or non-exclusive agreement to develop a specific type of enzyme," explains Jørgen Rode, marketing director for the detergent industry at Novozymes. "For example, a detergent manufacturer could come to us and say they would like us to develop a protease specially suitable for their particular formulation in specific washing conditions. We have a large bank of microorganisms and can generate more diversity if necessary by using state-of-the-art technology. We can screen what works and what doesn't by using different assays. In short, we can usually find the enzyme a customer wants. ... Partnering projects fuel innovation," says Rode.

He points out that the detergent industry is different from most other industry segments served by Novozymes. A few large players dominate it. The size of these multinational companies calls for a special approach and a global team at Novozymes under a strategic account manager normally handles them. This close relationship with major customers can form the basis for a close cooperation on research and development.

Learning Processes

Customer service processes are managed through customer ecosystem technology. Inquiries about products' functions and other inquiries provide a source of information that will help Novozymes learn from experience even more effectively than it has in the past.

By examining patterns in the problems and issues that customers have with Novozymes products, the company hopes to gain insight on new versions or applications for its existing products. Customer "care-abouts" are examined to learn what concerns customers have regarding product attributes or new functions that they are looking for.

Necessary Infrastructure

Customer relationship management was the original objective when Novozymes began deploying customer ecosystem technology. Although much of what was deployed originated from the need to deploy a sales management process, Novozymes quickly recognized that the need to provide common customer data was not just a sales function need.

"Anyone in the company that had day-to-day contact with customers is a user of the customer management system, whether they are in sales, marketing, technical services, or customer service," says Thorkil Tøttrup, Manager of CRM, Novozymes North America. Access to customer information throughout the company is intended to provide a higher-quality customer experience regardless of an individual's specific job description.

Novozymes has customers throughout the world and the company has pursued them by providing sales offices and distribution services locally. In order to coordinate relationship around the world, network infrastructure needed to be more than just e-mail and file sharing. Customer data became infrastructure for ensuring that the various regional offices felt and acted as part of the overall team.

Strategic Business Architecture

Critical elements for Novozymes' technology architecture are three main components: the customer management system, the corporate Web site and customer extranet, and the enterprise resource planning system.

The customer management system is currently deployed as an internal management system, coordinating sales process, activity, and contact information. Large accounts, like the Procter & Gambles of the world, receive direct contact with account managers, which has been the traditional mode of contact since the company started in the 1940s.

Novozymes' award-winning e-commerce site and outstanding Web site are intended to provide access to information about enzymes and the company, extending the key capabilities of transaction and engagement to customers by the Internet. Lower-volume customers are provided direct access to product information and online ordering capability through the e-commerce site.

While each of these systems has been deployed separately and in fact they are separate applications, great care has been given to ensure that necessary customer information is integrated throughout each system. For example, since the e-commerce site accesses the main ERP system, online transactions are recorded in the same core system as offline transactions. The loop is closed with the sales organization, by feeding sales history and customer information from the enterprise resource planning system to the demand management system.

Consistency

Enzymes are technical products that are used to modify or change the properties of other ingredients in a variety of processes. The science behind the enzyme business is complex, making it dangerous to have wide variation in the customer management process, because this could easily result in problems with expectations of product performance. Among other things, including the core desire to improve sales performance, this was a primary driver for implementing a standard sales process for Novozymes. The movement to develop and enhance the sales process started in 1996 in the North American sales operations. Once the sales process was defined, Novozymes selected a software system to help with the creation of a system that could manage its customer information and its sales process. Due to a variety of circumstances, the implementation of technology didn't begin for almost three years.

The goal of the sales process system was to coach sales and customer management staff through a standard process to ensure quality and consistency and to create more accurate forecasts for the enzyme production process. Achieving consistency has not meant that Novozymes salespeople act like clones, however. Says Tøttrup, "We provide a basic path that ensures quality and guides sales people through basic steps. Whether they take a train or car or bicycle to get to the end destination, we are flexible about."

Demand Driven Strategy: Novozymes' Customer Ecosystem Alignment

Customer Ecosystem Dynamics

With the strength of Novozymes in its market environment (at 45% market share), the company has a great deal of sway over market dynamics (see Figure 11-2).

Traditional markets are becoming mature, and some enzyme products are becoming commodities. Many customers are relatively passive, preferring to allow Novozymes to provide expert guidance for product- or solution-related issues.

Large manufacturers require a close association to enhance their products' position in the marketplace. Their desire for control in the relationship can be significant. Some key customers take the role of activist or collaborator.

The business environment continues to involve distributors, who are required to serve niche industry markets or specific geographies. As well, many low-frequency, low-volume customers are still effectively serviced through distributors.

Adaptive Strategies

Novozymes has significant influence on the industry context due to its technical leadership and dominant market share position. As the context leader for the industrial enzymes business, Novozymes continually steps up performance pressure for its competitors. As the leader of the customer ecosystem, Novozymes finds a key source of resource synergy is leveraging customer knowledge for the creation of new enzyme performance requirements.

The Novozymes brand is intended to convey scientific leadership that enables customers to improve the performance of their own products. The brand is somewhat loosely defined, which gives it an adaptive framework to respond to market conditions.

Information Technology

Novozymes has chosen to create best-of-breed applications for traditional business functions and then integrate these applications. A separate system exists for sales and customer service, for Web information, and for e-commerce. However, Novozymes has worked hard to integrate these systems to appear seamless to internal users and to the outside users.

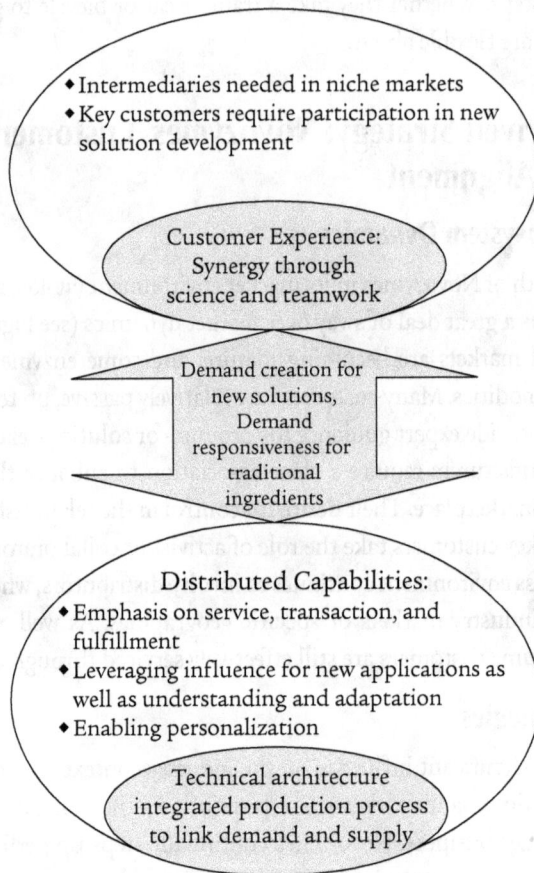

```
• Intermediaries needed in niche markets
• Key customers require participation in new
  solution development

          Customer Experience:
          Synergy through
          science and teamwork

          Demand creation for
          new solutions,
          Demand
          responsiveness for
          traditional
          ingredients

          Distributed Capabilities:
• Emphasis on service, transaction, and
  fulfillment
• Leveraging influence for new applications as
  well as understanding and adaptation
• Enabling personalization

          Technical architecture
          integrated production process
          to link demand and supply
```

Figure 11-2. Novozymes: Environmentally sensitive

Novozymes' culture appears to be a major competitive advantage in the marketplace. Sensitivity to markets, to the general business environment, and to customers and the accompanying rapid response to issues and customer needs enables the company to provide exceptional customer experience and value.

Distributed Capabilities

Particularly adept at understanding market and customer requirements through its involvement in research and dissemination of information, Novozymes is able to influence its customers and position itself for lasting demand. The company also is structured effectively to adapt to customer requirements.

Distributed Capabilities	Capability = Competency + Technology-Enabled Activity
Positioning Capabilities	Engage—Highly sensitive culture in the organization + business systems that enable the most appropriate people to address customer needs and allow them to be rapidly dispatched to customer requirements
	Adapt—Customer teams are accustomed to change as customer needs change + systems to relay those changes to management and peers
	Understand—Highly sensitive culture + customer service applications to capture and disseminate information
	Influence—Organization is accustomed to being the market leader + business systems push information to consumers through Internet and sales people to enable influence
Interaction Capabilities	Fulfill—Fulfillment linked from online transaction system to ERP system
	Service—Capabilities for enabling after-sales support triggered through internal customer management system
	Transact—Transaction capabilities enabled online and through distributors
	Personalize—Interfaces can be customized online, products can be personalized through development process and customer interaction

Figure 11-4. Novozymes' capabilities

Business Impact

Novozymes is looking for specific impacts in terms of customer satisfaction and increased sales revenue. The creation of the customer service and e-commerce systems began without specific targets for increased revenue or increased satisfaction ratings. At this point, Novozymes is trying to measure the impact without the benefit of baseline measures.

A veteran of both enterprise resource planning systems implementations and now demand management systems, Tøttrup has a unique insight on how to ensure successful implementation of Novozymes' demand management system.

The primary difference between the customer-oriented systems and the financial- and production-oriented systems is the potential for non-use. "With an ERP system, once you roll it out, the user doesn't really have a choice not to use the application," says Tøttrup. Invoices must be posted, orders and accounts must be updated, and there is really no opportunity for variation. Tøttrup contrasts this with a customer- and demand-oriented application, where the biggest challenge is "you don't have to use it. The business is not going stop working if a salesperson does not record a call or the service rep doesn't record a customer inquiry."

But in the long term, the more strategic application is the one that is most easily ignored in the short term. "The way that you treat your real assets, customers, and knowledge is really more important than the way you book your invoices," says Tøttrup.

What do you do about this? Tøttrup has developed a business architecture that includes real responsibilities for system maintenance and use for the long haul. Following the implementation of technology, the real work begins. Responsibility for use of technology and information will be pushed to the key business users, including sales, marketing, and customer service managers. Formal responsibility for helping peers use the system will be given to a number of "super-users" in each office of the Novozymes organization. In addition, regional champions will have a more senior role of ensuring use and application of the system in decision-making situations.

12

Implementing Strategy in a Customer Ecosystem

n ecosystem is an intertwined, interrelated biological structure, which exists despite being constantly somewhere between total chaos and stagnation. The ecosystem metaphor for business and customer management is particularly apt for emphasizing the need for balance or, at least, the pursuit of balance.

In previous chapters, we have described the process for building a customer ecosystem and how four organizations have approached the ecosystem issue. This chapter shows that different approaches to seeking balance among customer demands, ecosystem dynamics, and business requirements ultimately achieve similar ecosystem ends.

The first perspective that we will examine is the balanced scorecard management system, at work in a well-known retail organization. The second perspective is a modification of the balanced scorecard approach, adapted to fit a small regional bank that built an ecosystem of demand for its financial products and services through the smart use of technology and a keen understanding of customer activism.

Deploying Customer Ecosystem Strategy Through Balanced Measures

In 1992 Harvard Business School professors Robert Kaplan and David Norton launched a management system they called the balanced scorecard. They believed that the key challenge with business today was not the formulation of effective strategy, but its implementation. In order for more companies to be more effective with strategy, measurements need to be broken down into bit-sized pieces that link measurable activity to the overall goals and strategy of the organization.

The balanced scorecard framework identifies four key areas of measurement: financial, customer, internal, and learning and growth. Companies like Exxon/Mobil, CIGNA Insurance, and Chemical (Chase) Retail Bank in the United States have employed a balanced scorecard approach. In Canada, Nova Scotia Power, Equifax, and others have successfully improved their business using Kaplan and Norton's principles.

The approach for defining the dependencies and linkages between business objectives and implementation tactics is really quite simple. Through a process of asking *dependency*-revealing questions like "If we are to achieve an increase in return on managed assets, what must be in place?" management is able to determine what activities and linkages underpin the primary objectives.

A second core premise of the balanced scorecard approach is that nothing really happens in business without measurement. Each element of the strategy implementation framework requires a measurement that is related to activity and that this measurement would be linked to performance evaluation of employees.

Example 1: Mobil North America

Kaplan and Norton's most successful example of the balanced scorecard in action is Mobil North America Marketing and Refining. This division of worldwide conglomerate Mobil Oil (now Exxon/Mobil) was a money-losing, mostly indistinguishable participant of the retail gasoline market through most of the early 1990s.

Their objective was to improve return on capital employed to a respectable level—12%. A simple enough goal, but without the underlying business objectives and activity linkages in place there was little for the company to latch onto to achieve any amount of change.

Based on the framework of defining objectives for financial, customer, operational, and learning and growth, Mobil was able to define the linkages that led it to a dramatic turnaround in business performance. Linking these characteristics for Mobil provided an easily understood roadmap of the behaviors and principles for employees and for partners to understand.

What is truly remarkable from our perspective about this example is the creation of several core elements of a customer ecosystem. From a customer perspective, Mobil conducted extensive research to understand the segments that were the most attractive targets for it to work with. It identified three core groups of customers who were using its stations with regularity and intensity. For these customers, it devised a customer retention program utilizing technology. The Speedpass enables customers to buy gas and food and other on-the-go items without waiting in line at a checkout.

Prior to its strategy implementation exercise, Mobil had significant challenges with its dealer affiliate network in terms of relationship and apparent goal divergence. For example, Mobil affiliates were forced to compete with regional or independent no-frills dealers, because the company had no core strategy for differentiation or customer retention. This often meant that the Mobil affiliates were often caught in a margin squeeze. Somewhat unaware of this conflict, Mobil had on occasion tried to download marketing and promotion expense for unfocused general campaigns. Through the process of setting objectives for customers, Mobil managers came to realize that a critical success factor was to have a win-win relationship with their dealer affiliate network.

Whether management knew it or not, Mobil built an ecosystem of demand by understanding the drivers of customer experience as well as the economics of indirect demand.

- First, Mobil NA understood that ease of transaction, that is, the ability to *react* to customer demand, was paramount to a customer not very interested in a closer relationship in terms of two-way flow of information or increased knowledge or connection. No, Mobil learned that, so long as it could react most efficiently to the things that its customers wanted—and wanted right now—it would capture repeat purchases. This represented true adaptation to the customer ecosystem, rather than considering this a relationship that the customer doesn't really want and the supplier would just waste capital by trying to enhance.
- Second, Mobil created indirect demand that suited the economic models of its partners, the retail outlets. By combating the lower revenues its partners had experienced with a more effective supporting revenue stream, Mobil was able to create a degree of indirect demand that helped to support demand for its core business, which was simply to sell gasoline. The indirect demand that supported its core business was the demand for soft goods, food, and other convenience items.

Lessons from the Balanced Scorecard

The balanced scorecard is effective in ensuring that return on investment is achieved. Like any strategy, customer ecosystem strategy doesn't succeed unless it is properly implemented. An ecosystem scorecard helps focus organizations on both internal and external objectives that ensure an integrated implementation of strategy.

Balanced Scorecard Elements	Traditional Business Issues	Customer Ecosystem Business Issues
Financial	Return on Capital Employed	Return on Capital Employed + Return on Ecosystem Capital
Customer	Customer Satisfaction	Customer Satisfaction, Customer Experience, Partner Experience
Operational	Organizational Processes	Organizational and Extended Capabilities + Business/Technical Architecture
Learning	Organizational Learning	Building Understanding Capability

Figure 12-1. Balanced scorecard and perspectives on issues

Applying the Balanced Scorecard in a Customer Ecosystem

Creating a fully integrated business and technology strategy was the goal of small company located a few blocks away from Pivotal's main office in Vancouver, Canada.

Example 2: North Shore Credit Union

North Shore Credit Union is a small, community banking institution located in North Vancouver. Its 30,000 members are mostly local residents and small businesses, but it makes a significant investment in the creation of a highly networked, integrated approach to managing customers, strategy, and the business using an open, flexible technology approach.

Small companies like NSCU cannot afford to make a lot of wrong moves in a highly competitive marketplace like the banking industry. Through a strategic planning process, key pressure points were identified that would ensure viability of the company and launch it on the route to growth.

Between 1996 and 1999, former CEO Jane Milner and her whole team at NSCU created their own version of Kaplan and Norton's balanced scorecard. They knew that the linkages between financial objectives and other measurements were critical for a small company. In order to achieve the benefits for the membership, they needed to create a big shining light that their members and staff could relate to.

For the credit union to be viable, the most important goal was growth of financial assets under management. This focus is not novel in any way in the financial sector, but in the cooperative branch of that sector, many credit unions believe themselves to be successful if they have more members. The problem was, for NSCU at least, that it wasn't as hard to get members as it was to get members to keep their money with the credit union. While having 30,000 members is respectable, most members held their investments and loans at other institutions, leaving very little in the way of deposits and other assets at the credit union.

The strategic planning process identified four areas of the organization that needed constant attention: financials, membership, people, and learning. NSCU created specific measures and specific actions that would help it achieve its overall goals of growing its businesses.

First and foremost, NSCU targeted assets under management. In order for the credit union to pass along better services and at reasonable costs, additional revenue from financial assets was necessary. Milner felt that a reasonable increase target, though certainly a stretch, was 10% per year.

Wellness

While the core focus of NSCU's business, increase the assets under management, was completely clear to most employees, the route to doing this was not so straightforward. There are relatively few ways to compete for assets in the personal and business banking sector. No-frills, virtual banks like ING Direct have created a business that has very few products and almost no physical locations, keeping costs down and providing attractive savings rates. The chartered banks and larger credit unions have the capability to manage a broad range of products to appeal to a broad range of customer needs.

"We decided to act differently. Instead of adopting a product focus, we made the decision to concentrate on the concept of overall financial wellness," says

Milner. From NSCU's perspective, there are four parts to financial wellness: banking, borrowing, investing, and protecting (for example, insurance). Financial wellness varies according to a customer's life stage. Different products are needed in each of these four areas at different life stages. NSCU's value proposition is to assist members with all four of these areas and, by doing that, take a leading position in being a wellness partner in a collaborative customer relationship setting.

The Jumping-Off Point

In the early part of 1999, NSCU got serious about growth. Some operational costs were down due to improved ATM, bank card, and call center use, but the growth was still not there.

At this point, it began planning and evaluating the potential for customer relationship management systems. Targeting the right customers to grow their "share of wallet" had to be the right approach for the small organization; new CEO Chris Catliff was convinced of this.

The plan for the implementation began to take shape with the help of consulting staff from Pivotal. Taking the general direction of managed asset growth, Pivotal facilitated implementations through goal-setting and process change workshops.

"We knew what it was going to feel like, in the branches and for the customers," says Elaine McHarg, who was Senior Vice President of Sales and Marketing. But what they worked out was the specific targets that would ensure the right fit with the company culture and that no missteps would be made.

Like many companies, NSCU knew that this was the right thing at an emotional level. "We knew in the gut that we had to do this," says Milner. "You have to understand that an investment of the magnitude we were contemplating in software and technology was the equivalent of three new branches," she explains. "For our membership and board of directors to do this, we had to ensure payback."

Developing an Ecosystem Culture

Through 1997 and 1998, NSCU worked to develop its network of ATMs and to develop the local branches. In 1997, telephone banking was offered and in 1998, customers could complete routine banking transactions online.

McHarg describes the situation: "In 1995, we had only 22% of customers using bank cards. From our experience in other banks, we knew how much value we could add and how dramatically we could improve operations by leveraging technology, particularly the Internet."

Through this period, McHarg worked to change the thinking of this traditional organization to think of the Internet and how other technologies could be used to improve the organization.

"We would have marketing and sales meeting, and some of the team members got to the point that they knew what I was going to say next: 'That's great, but how will this relate to the Internet?'" laughs McHarg. Building the culture over time was necessary because of the type of staff that was working for the credit union. Many staff are local residents who believe in the concept of a shared financial cooperative and were not so enthusiastic about building a business.

Building the "Builders"

One key element of NSCU's strategy focused on membership by improving member targeting. NSCU undertook extensive analysis of the linkages between its business operations and its membership base. Through this analysis, it identified a segment it called "Builders," men and women between 30 and 45 who were, as McHarg describes, "establishing their careers, building assets and responsibilities." Members in this segment were the most likely to require a mortgage—a financial commitment most people take seriously. But they were also most likely to hold that mortgage at another bank or credit union.

It was clear to NSCU that it needed to "change the rules"—it would no longer find it acceptable for members to automatically renew at another bank; it wanted to get its fair share. A number of core activities were designed to capture the attention of the target segment and then add a unique kind of value. NSCU needed to reconfigure the relationship with a customer that typically acted as the value leader in the relationship.

NSCU developed a membership profiling approach that transformed its paper-based system into a systematized cohesive membership management system. Too often the paper-based system was in too many people's hands. "Over the past few years, we added new sales and service channels: online banking, brokerage, an after-hours call center staffed with financial advisors," explains CEO Catliff. In order to capture all of the information on customers, it needed to be in one place. "With the member profiling system in a shared database, we knew we would gain some efficiencies, but the real goal was for targeted sales and marketing." Figure 12-2 shows NCSU's new approach utilized many key customer capabilties.

NSCU's Big Bet

"We bet $1.8 million on our plan to improve the business overall through improved customer relationship management," says former CEO Milner. "It was

Customer Capability	NCSU's Competency	Technology-Enabled Activity
Understanding	Customer targeting	Profile data entry into CRM System
Engaging	Asking for customer mortgage quotation	System reminder based on renewal date
Adapting	Recognition of changing demographics and need to change offers	Regular offers sent to clients daily rather than mass mailing/advertising
Influencing	Influencing customers to switch financial institution	Mostly offline persuasion
Personalizing	Specifically targeted local "builders"	Profile data plus automated processes to contact with the right offer
Transacting	Ability to provide range of services tailored to target ecosystem	Online activity to enable customers to shop various services
Services	Ability to provide range of services tailored to target ecosystem	Online activity to enable customers to shop various services
Finding	Ability to provide range of services tailored to target ecosystem	Online activity to enable customers to shop various services

Figure 12-2. NCSU's new approach

the single largest investment ever approved by the board of directors. In fact, with pre-implementation revenues of around $2.0 million, this investment gone the wrong way would put the credit union out of business.

"We could not afford to fail in this implementation, for a variety of obvious reasons," intones Milner. Not that this was an edge-of-the-seat situation. By adopting parts of the balanced scorecard approach to aligning measurement and strategy, NSCU had measurements for each of the four key elements of a balanced scorecard: financial, customer, internal business process, and learning and growth.

The decision makers at NSCU knew that, while a credit union may be as patient an organization as there is in the financial sector, they needed to improve their competitive position rapidly. From McHarg's viewpoint, "the question was that if we could only achieve a few of these in 15-18 months, how should we get there? And really, when you think about it, to have a few major achievements from

Balanced Scorecard Elements	NSCU's Targets	Ecosystem Business Issues	NSCU's Extended Goals
Financial	Return on Capital Employed: 12%	Return on Capital Employed + Return on Ecosystem Capital	Leverage Internet resource, leverage financial wellness partners
Customer	Customer Satisfaction and Retention: Increased number of mortgage customers	Customer Satisfaction, Customer Experience, Partner Experience	Build customer wellness experience concept, create partners for "wellness"
Operational	Organizational Processes: Specific goals for conducting wellness reviews	Organizational and Extended Capabilities + Business/Technical Architecture	Create competency and infrastructure to deliver "wellness" activity
Learning	Organizational Learning: Specific targets for learning about the customer	Building Understanding Capability	Understand the needs of key "builders"

Figure 12-3. Balanced scorecard and NSCU issues and goals

an initiative like this is pretty good."

One of the major milestones that combined many of the top three areas of the balanced scorecard was the target of increasing sales of mortgages. This seemingly simple measure linked the overall financial goal with customer goals and with internal business process. Each of these goals was achieved through synergy between the staff and management of NSCU and the new aspects of automated process and integrated customer data (see Figure 12-3).

One simple measure for this organization was not enough. Said Catliff, "I should also mention that each metric cascaded back into other pieces ... attitudes, knowledge, technical skills ... it all worked together."

Implementing the System

What makes the North Shore Credit Union implementation different from many customer-management technology installations is that it focused on business planning as much as on system implementation planning.

Initial sessions focused on the profiling system to ensure that it was useful throughout the various channels of the organization. While that may be a common thing, the focus and measure of success was "How is this going to change the business?" at each step along the way.

"We knew, of course," says McHarg, "that we wanted to facilitate process and increase customer satisfaction and relationship and all that, but the trick was how to drive an additional $70 million of assets under administration. This was our goal for the project."

Some of the old business processes, for example, had to be abandoned in order to achieve the business results. As a community credit union, geography has traditionally defined some part of the relationship with customers. But NSCU chose not to go this route. Explains Allen, "In setting up our system, we made the conscious decision to concentrate on member-defined households, not address-defined households. This was a big decision for us."

Instead, North Shore Credit Union focused on creating automated processes through improved data. "Our customer profile has two parts: a mini and a full profile," says Allen. "The full profile has nine questions. When a customer opens an account, we ask that person if they own their home, if they have a mortgage, and if so, what institution is it with and when is it up? They don't have to tell us all this, of course, but most want to." Profile information can be gathered by anyone in the organization: call center, brokerage, financial advisors, or frontline staff.

The customer profile information enables automatic system activity to place offers in front of customers that are appropriate to their life stage. For example, a mortgage renewal date for someone in the "Builders" segment is used to create a letter and schedule a follow-up call to discuss his or her mortgage renewal date.

Automation of processes is not revolutionary. However, measurement of this specific activity to ensure that this one key element was on the right track *and* that it meant something to employees is unique. Explains McHarg, "We took early measurements to reassure staff and manage the transition. We compared the sales results from Q4 1999—pre-implementation—to those of Q1 2000—post-implementation. We expected our senior financial advisors' sales revenue to increase by 10% to 15%. It increased 20%."

Understanding Capabilities

Employees have had tremendous benefit from the system, from improved personal performance to increased insight. The key benefits from a learning perspective have been in the form of "aha's"—observations or insights that are counter to common beliefs.

In a personal relationship business like banking, a company relies on customer-facing staff for their judgment of each customer's attractiveness. With a solid process to learn about customers, this judgment is now based on more fact than gut feel. "After the implementation, it was great to hear anecdotal stories from the financial advisors, ... what they found about customers' holdings at other institutions, for example," says McHarg. The advisors also developed a better understanding of customer goals and relationships.

Because of the change in the market approach, employees had to learn to work more closely among departments. For example, as marketing changed from a traditional campaign-based focus, the marketing department gained insight into customers on a more personal level.

"The marketing department was actually the biggest promoters of the wellness program internally," explains Allen. "In order to really make it work, we sought constant feedback from members because the campaigns were now run on a constant basis."

While this is a small company, the linkage of the sales role—represented in the position of senior financial advisor—and the marketing department was previously fairly loose. The linkage between the marketing stimulus—for example, the mortgage renewal letter—and the business response—higher sales for the senior financial advisor—was now very direct. "Marketing and sales really started to function as a team," says Allen.

13

Transforming Non-Profit Ecosystems

Non-Profit Ecosystems Have Different Forms of Demand

A non-profit ecosystem may be very similar to a customer ecosystem in terms of the linkages among social organizations and a range of participants: members, donors, and other benefactors. The differences is the nature of the relationship, of course, from one of pure economics or an exchange of goods and services to a range of other motivations, like caregiving, community, or other common interests.

In terms of ecosystem characteristics, non-profit organizations like service groups, clubs, professions, and other voluntary organizations are even more like a biological system than markets and customers, for example.

Both ecosystems and non-profit organizations are self-organizing. Volunteer organizations, by their very nature, are self-organizing. Some are more structured and regimented than others, with bylaws, officers, presidents, and management.

The interactions within ecosystems and within non-profit networks each follow their own set of common, simple rules. For example, the United Way is a caring organization and, as its mandate implies, all activities related to this fundamental objective. When activities don't relate to the common, simple rules, then a non-profit organization will tend to become more erratic and less stable.

Ecosystems and non-profit organizations can experience rapid and accelerating change. Depending on the organization, membership in a group can grow rapidly and the direction of the non-profit organization can change rapidly. A large influx of new members can cause a traditional political party or non-profit organization to become something very different, almost overnight.

Smaller ecosystems embed to create larger ecosystems—just as smaller non-profit organizations embed to create larger organizations. Within a larger organization such as the Red Cross, which we will profile below, several smaller causes or events make up the overall organization. The Red Cross, for example deals with domestic disasters and events as well as international events including wars and natural disasters like earthquakes and floods. The organization needs coordination and inter-relationship of all of these activities.

The following section outlines one specific organization that has a non-profit ecosystem and uses technology effectively to coordinate the capabilities of that non-profit ecosystem.

The Red Cross/Red Crescent Movement

One of the most famous and oldest charities in the world, the Red Cross movement exists for humanitarian benefit in all parts of the earth. Originally established as a society that set codes of conduct and provided humanitarian relief in times of war, today the Federation of Red Cross and Red Crescent Societies supports the development of humanitarian activities by national societies. Whether it is emergency relief from natural disasters, the development of new social welfare initiatives, caring for refugees, or simply providing comfort for the vulnerable of any society, the Federation is there, offering the aid of Red Cross volunteers around the globe.

Today the Red Cross is a worldwide disaster relief organization with around 200 million volunteers who work in their own local communities. The main role of the Red Cross is to provide protection to victims of war and relief during times of natural disasters such as fires, floods, droughts, famine, and earthquakes.

Despite a famous name and a high level of public awareness, the Red Cross movement competes for charitable giving with more organizations than ever before. The non-profit environment for charitable giving is much more demanding and competitive, even as the need for contributions of leading charities like the Red Cross is greater than ever.

In Australia, each of the six states and two territories has separately established

Red Cross Societies. Within some of the state groups, different divisions may carry out different roles. This places the services and the caring volunteers close to where they are needed most, but at times it causes challenges in coordination.

Multiple Relationships

In order to coordinate the services offered, the Australian Red Cross is a network composed of many different participants in a variety of roles. Volunteers may help with delivering services such as Telecross, through which elderly people registered with the program may get a phone call each day to ensure that they can answer the phone and that they are not in any distress. Other volunteers may assist in the quarterly fundraising campaigns, like the Door Knock Appeal that runs annually in March. In addition to general volunteers, the ARC needs to coordinate health care workers and trainers for delivering CPR and first aid courses.

Of course, the Red Cross must develop relationships with the individuals who are willing and able to provide financial assistance. Consistent and effective care and handling of the financial donors is essential to the survival of organization. It is also the most demanding without some form of infrastructure and coordination. "Donors are extremely sensitive to how, when and what we ask for in terms of financial support," says Michael Stapleton, ARC Chief Information Officer. "Sometimes a donor would get requests for several different programs within a few short weeks and they already had told us that they only wished to contribute to international appeals, for example."

Coordination

Ensuring that appeal programs and other requests are coordinated was a monumental task for the organization. Donor information was held in a mainframe system offsite and was not easily accessed. Membership information would be held at local branches; with luck it would be held in a spreadsheet, but in some cases membership information would be in handwritten journals.

In the Australian Red Cross—New South Wales Annual Report, the faces of the volunteers, members, and donors are presented throughout. "People are our asset" goes the slogan. But the coordination of the people to help people was becoming monumental in difficulty.

In one division, for example, there were eight different databases. With six states and two territories, Stapleton estimates that there could have been as many as 64 separate sources of data on contacts and relationships. Implementing a relationship management system enabled each separate division to have access to a state-of-the-art technology tool that could operate all parts of the business.

"What we've done here transcends the technology tool," admits Stapleton. Coordinating the information on people and relationships has helped the societies in the states and divisions to become one organization.

Many specific software packages existed for fundraising, but they solved only one of the many problems that faced ARC. The organization is typified by diversity. The core activities that it needed to coordinate included donations, fundraising, events, volunteer activity, and recruitment. Starting with a core system that managed contacts and activities, ARC designed, built, and maintains a system customized to also cover membership and fundraising.

The Change Process

Volunteer organizations are notoriously difficult to coordinate—the mental image of "herding cats" comes to mind. The ARC, having made the decision to change how it operated across the country, now had to make it happen.

Implementing a new technology solution where none existed before appeared daunting at first. Basing all new technology on the common Microsoft platform ensured that resources could be found to maintain systems and that more people could access the technology. People were simply used to the same kinds of interfaces that they used in their own work and homes.

Leadership and commitment are critical to ARC's success. Getting agreement to go ahead with the implementation also could have been a problem. Regional interests and personal agendas might have killed the initiative, had the National Executive and leadership of each state not been unanimously behind the decision. From the top down, the Executive Committee of the Australian Red Cross knew that it was not sustainable to continue as it was.

Coordinated Appeals

With competition for donors extremely tough, ARC needed to ensure that it knew more about donors and it needed to manage the fundraising process more effectively.

With four appeals per year, ARC has been able to hone its processes and coordinate fundraising activities much more effectively with the new relationship management technology. Now it is able to target who is giving in what circumstances and ensuring that people who want to give only to specific programs are not approached for the wrong programs. In general, this makes for a more positive public image by ensuring that communications are coordinated.

This capability is changing the culture of the organization as well. In the past, volunteers or the executive of a division would just contact whomever they wished and whenever they wished. It just wasn't possible to coordinate any activities. Now, most requests are coordinated with other appeals and other communications to ensure consistency of message.

Applications That Anybody Can Use

Not-for-profit organizations have some unique challenges in terms of the human resources pool that corporations do not. The humble volunteer is absolutely essential to the success of any appeal or any of the other services offered by the ARC. The problem is that volunteers come and go, have varying computer skills, and have extremely little patience for difficult tasks when they are giving their free time to whatever worthwhile cause.

The Red Cross had some critical technology architecture needs that needed to be met in order to ensure that its relationship management system was successful. First, the system had to be easy to learn. Because of the Microsoft environment, new volunteers could find their way around the system in short order. Second, regardless of how well-meaning a volunteer might be, the organization could not afford to allow changes to records that should not be changed.

Measuring Benefit in a Nonprofit Environment

However difficult it is to measure payback in a nonprofit environment, there is specific proof of improvement in efficiency. The Telecross program, for example, coordinates a calling program to elderly people and other shut-ins. "The rostering for Telecross used to take four days to coordinate all the different lists and names," says Stapleton, "and now it takes about two hours."

Ensuring health care standards are met is one approach to measuring quality of life. In Australia companies are required to have people on staff trained in first aid and emergency procedures in the WorkCover program. In the past, there was really no way of knowing when someone's certificate of training had expired; it was really up to the individual to ensure that he or she got recertified. "Lives being as busy as they are today, people forget or push this kind of thing to the bottom of the list," acknowledges Stapleton. Not that the Red Cross is a watchdog, but it is useful to send reminder letters for people to get recertified. And it works. Enrollment and certifications in targeted programs are on the rise—just another reason to be sure that there is real benefit from their effort and investment in a technology that links volunteers, members, and the public to the important works of the Australian Red Cross.

14

Conclusion: How Customer Ecosystems Change Business Strategy and Practice

The changes in the business world have created many new opportunities for companies that embrace the concept of demand management in the customer ecosystem.

Transforming a business enterprise into a customer ecosystem requires companies to think about their industry sectors differently and to think about their business activities differently. Business people, management theorists, and educators need to think about the functions and the disciplines of business management differently in order to envision a more integrated way of doing business in a network environment.

As we discussed in the Chapter 1, a customer ecosystem is very different in character from a supply chain, even though they may actually be the same actual grouping of companies. Because of viewpoint and philosophic bent, the character of a company that deploys positioning and interaction capabilities to influence and adapt a customer ecosystem is very different from a company that seeks to control or regulate a supply chain.

Reinventing Industries

Looking at an industry as a customer ecosystem provides unique perspectives for creating sustainable demand for your own products and services. By viewing the ultimate customers' experience from which you derive your own demand, you may uncover opportunities to change the way things are done.

Is this the same as channel innovation, such as what Dell Computers has done in direct marketing to consumers? No doubt Dell has taken major steps in creating relationships directly with customers, but it hasn't influenced the influencers as may be necessary in the long run.

The nature of demand management is to care and feed all the participants that affect the network. Companies that seek to understand the extended requirements of their customers and perhaps their customers' customers will build a customer ecosystem with some staying power.

World Sports Distribution Network

The aftermath of the dot-com debacle has left many people a little gun-shy about companies designed to capitalize on Internet capability. World Sports Distribution Network is a start-up company that has identified a key opportunity to revolutionize the golf industry through customer ecosystems. It also illustrates the critical linkage of demand and supply chain thinking.

Zachary Sabel, the chief technology officer (CTO) of WSDN, a participant in entrepreneurial start-ups such as Cardio Response, was approached about three years ago to create a dot-com specializing in women's golf apparel. By any standard, the level of service for women's golf products and apparel in pro shops is typically less than adequate. A women's online golf source seemed like a good idea, but timing-wise, late 1999 and early 2000 was not conducive to pure-play start-up e-commerce. Earlier entrants, like Chipshot.com, were struggling and many recently have gone out of business.

The apparent opportunity in the women's golf market stemmed from a much greater problem. As golfers know, the level of service at a golf pro shop varies from excellent to adequate to abysmal. The source of this problem is that there is a skill mismatch in relation to golf professionals being left in charge of the pro shop. "Somewhere along the way, the golf industry has neglected to modernize the business of selling products, while modernizing every other aspect of the sport," says Sabel.

The Pro Shop Network

Of the 16,000 golf pro shops in the United States, only a very few crack the million-dollar mark in sales. Basic economics tells us that some form of distribution channel is necessary to supply these businesses with apparel and golf equipment and typically this is in the form of manufacturers' reps with multiple lines of products.

The explosion of product suppliers in the golf market, driven by the rapid rise in popularity of golf as a social and cultural phenomenon, further compounds the complexity of the relationships that the golf pro must manage.

Consider the golf pro. Millions of golfers perceive that the life of a golf pro must be fairly idyllic. And for the most part, giving lessons and participating in tournaments are rewarding experiences. The combined experiences of managing, stocking, or even staffing the pro shop are easily lowest on the list of reasons to become a golf pro.

The Customer Experience

Pro shop customers are typically the members of the golf club or, less frequently, guests or visitors. At private clubs, the golf pro will get to know the customers quite well and consequently is able to provide good service and a positive relationship experience. Even then, with 80% of goods sold in a golf shop being customized in some fashion, a heightened opportunity for service is clearly apparent. Take custom clubs, for example. Golfers frequently wait for six to eight weeks for a custom club to be made and delivered. The golf product suppliers struggle to keep pace with overall demand from the likes of Golf Day and other leading retailers and unfortunately have an even more difficult time providing custom clubs for thousands of individuals through tiny pro shops across the continent.

Strategic Applications

Golf pro shops have the typical pattern of disparate systems and processes for solving specific business process issues. A point-of-sale system is necessary to sell and account for products. A tee-booking system, which may be paper-based, is required to ensure coordination of the main business resource. An inventory system is required for keeping track of what's in the pro shop; it may also be paper-based. And, finally, the purchasing system may only be the telephone call to the favored reps that the pro shop typically deals with.

Not being business-oriented at heart, the golf pro is not concerned with the great opportunities for customer retention and share of wallet, so a critical but overlooked strategic application appears to be the customer management system.

WSDN Strategy

WSDN is attempting to reconfigure the golf customer ecosystem. Its core business proposition is to enable golf pro shops to manage the business side of the business, by providing the application infrastructure and purchasing capability to pro shop managers who have neither the skill nor the inclination to spend more time on shop management. As WSDN manages its customers, the golf pros, it aggregates demand, smoothing the flow of demand for products as a wholesaler but with additional capabilities to enable customization and business management. By working with WSDN, the golf shop is able to provide things like embroidered club shirts or custom clubs more responsively.

In the longer term, WSDN will enable the golf pro to better manage the relationship side of the business by creating the capability to manage customer information more effectively and even to learn from customers at a higher level than previously possible. Transformation of customer information will enable the golf pro to be better at anticipating customer needs and to provide products that fit the profile of his or her own customers. Ultimately, this will create a demand pattern that ensures that individuals' needs are addressed and aggregate customer ecosystem needs are addressed.

Rather than being a "dot-com," WSDN is following a distributed capabilities approach. Not only does WSDN provide online order and inventory management capabilities to pro shops, it provides warehousing, distribution, and customization services. With 50,000 square feet of warehousing space and state-of-the-art embroidering machinery, WSDN can respond to orders in days rather than weeks.

The Transformed Experience

For golf pros, the role of salesperson and shopkeeper is the least rewarding and perhaps the one they are least equipped for. WSDN offers them a relatively painless experience from a purchasing perspective. Online ordering, personalized inventory management, and faster, more responsive customization capabilities provide greater value to their customers with the ultimate benefit of improve business management of the golf shop.

The experience of the customer should also be improved. Custom products like fitted clubs are often a decision that takes some time to make, in part because it takes so long to take delivery. With rapid delivery capability, the customer may be more inclined to order a competitively priced custom club. A more up-to-date selection of fashionable apparel emblazoned with the course insignia could result from effective inventory management and make-to-order processes. The bad experiences faced by women golfers identified earlier may also be alleviated.

The Transformed Industry

How is this a demand management industry? WSDN approaches the golf industry from the golfers' perspective. Demand for golf apparel originates where golfers congregate: at the golf course. While big box stores are outstanding for supplying the fanatical independent golfer, the pro shop remains viable for its ability to supply the expertise and relationship necessary for critical decisions like custom clubs and for the community experience of club membership. Enhancing the experience of the golfer and the golf pro through technology and through effective business strategy creates a customer ecosystem that benefits the entire system.

Transforming Process

The importance of process in traditional marketing, sales, and customer service is understated and misunderstood. The traditional academic approach is functional and tactical. Managing customers has traditionally been a role for marketers, but marketing has been ineffective in leading the way. Regis McKenna, author of "Real-Time Marketing" (*Harvard Business Review*, July-August 1995) and the brains behind the successful technology marketing strategies employed by Apple and others, said in an interview in *Business 2.0* in October 2000 ("The End of Marketing"): "The marketing function is being marginalized to advertising and PR. You'll find in most companies that the person called vice president of marketing is really a 'marcom' person." The cult of marketing has reduced itself by heavy involvement in the creation of glitzy advertising and communications programs, neglecting the real work of marketing.

Today customer management occurs in many parts of the organization because of this failing and needs to be reunited: call centers manage customer support, sales teams manage customer acquisition, and marketing manages prospecting and advertising, independently of each other and the rest of the organization.

Integration of the functions is possible through unification on the enterprise demand management process. The capabilities of the organization for capturing demand are embodied in the demand-linking processes outlined in this book. Working together on the process for managing the demand development and retention process should enable companies to create new and unique ways of generating growth and revenue.

Transforming Business Disciplines

If old theories for understanding environment and customers are not adequate, then the whole function of managing demand through sales, service, and marketing is under significant pressure. Being involved in both business and technical education, for business students, employees, and customers, we have gained an appreciation for a key problem for businesses today: finding employees with both

159

technical capability and a creative bent for demand management and customer relationships.

Many people agree that the separation of technology and business management disciplines is a remnant of old school command-and-control organizational thinking. David Foote, managing partner at leading IT organization and staffing consulting firm Foote Partners, LLC, believes that "seven to 10 years from now, there will be no information technology organization as we know it today."[1] Rather, there will be teams of business technologists—MBA types with experience and knowledge in technology as well as some business disciplines.

Executives agree that the convergence of technology and business is hampering companies' ability to capitalize on new business opportunities. And executives are voting with their checkbook. Recently, the Wharton School of Business launched an e-business executive program wherein a four-week (non-consecutive) program cost almost $50,000 per participant and drew 35 executives.

The next phase of the Internet is one of synergy and complementarities with offline resources for business purposes will be about customer engagement and an expanding customer experience. As veterans of the customer relationship management wars, we recognize that few companies have been able to truly create the meaningful personal engagement that the CRM and one-to-one marketing school of thought have advocated.

The metaphor for the customer ecosystem is an organism. The ecosystem is made up of parts that, in themselves, are as physical as the chemical compounds that make up an organism. But in aggregate, these parts become fluid and interactive and above all not predictable....

Customer Ecosystems and One-to-One Marketing

The customer relationship management movement really took off with the contribution of B. Joseph Pine II, Don Peppers, and Martha Rogers and their seminal work "Do You Want to Keep Your Customers Forever?" (*Harvard Business Review*, March-April 1995). Many parts of the one-to-one philosophy remain central to the customer ecosystem proposition. Yet evolution is necessary, and we have build on many of the core concepts of one-to-one marketing, particularly the concept of the learning relationship, further refining it into some defined business processes, business architecture, and key strategic elements.

A critical distinction of the ecosystem concept from the one-to-one concept is the influence of the partners, intermediaries, incorporating a broader environment and it's corresponding complexity. The complexity of the customer ecosystem necessitates a move from "one-to-one" thinking to "many-to-many" thinking, that is, many relationships between customer and suppliers of various kinds, as well as partners of various kinds must be managed at the same time.

Demand-Driven and Market-Driven Strategy

At the heart of the ecosystem concept is the close engagement of customer and corporation. The concept that strategy follows customer needs and responds to market conditions through effective business process is increasingly recognized as an effective way to do business. This concept, known as *market-driven strategy*, evolved out of the marketing orientation work done by George Day at the Wharton School of Business.

Among his many important contributions, Day recommends that companies need to adopt a process perspective on customer relationships and on market-sensing. These are critical insights for companies and many of Pivotal's customers have adopted some of the principles.

The customer ecosystem concept embeds the technology and marketing process as a unified element with our concept of capabilities. We echo this concept in our assertion that the customer ecosystem is both physical and conceptual. Most marketers, including Day, have not been able to knit marketing process, strategy, and technology together as it is in a customer ecosystem.

Demand Orientation

Owing in origin to the concept of customer or market orientation, some organizations are evolving to a broader concept of external orientation. In this book we profile several companies that demonstrate a willingness to embrace a broader concept of market relationships; we call it *demand orientation*.

A demand orientation means that a company acknowledges the fluid and connected nature of the organization and its customers, partners, and suppliers. At the center of the organization is the customer. The associated network elements are involved in stimulating the demand for a product and/or service. Companies with this orientation employ strategies that both create demand and respond to demand. And in some cases they illustrate how activities within their network serve to create a broad concept of their business purpose, which is translated for the public in the concept of a "brand."

There are seven critical things you need to do to create a demand orientation for your business.

1. Understand Complexity

We believe that most industries are dynamic and complex. If you are unsure or don't agree, we challenge you to map the potential sources of change, the potential new economic entities that disintermediate and reconfigure your market structure.

Focus on the potential triggers of demand to understand and perhaps influence the next wave of market change. New technology can create a new basis of competition, but so much of it is related to sentiment and application.

2. Define Your Customer Experience

At the center of a business ecosystem, there is a customer. And this customer is looking for something unique and valuable in a business relationship within today's network economy.

Even though we have outlined many customer roles, and the demands of customers may change rapidly, the risk of not defining a compelling experience for one customer and getting it right for that customer is that you will not get it right for any customers. Appealing to the customers' senses means connecting with a series of intangible relationship elements: connection, commitment, contribution, excitement, and ultimately the customers' sense of value.

3. Build the Capabilities to Manage Multiple, New Customer Roles

New customer roles—like advocate, asset, activist, etc.—require new technology-enabled activities to ensure effective response so that targeted customer experience is delivered. Demand management capabilities must be able to manage:

- Multi-channel interactions: Web chat, IP voice, e-mail, voice, and fax-based
- Personalization, profile management, and dynamic delivery of Web content and organizational capabilities
- The ability to access demand management data anytime, anywhere, on any device
- The ability to deliver effective transaction processing, fulfillment, shipping, and billing, for accelerated market demand
- Engagement capabilities like needs analysis, advisory or guided selling, and complex configuration

4. Create an Organizational Capability to Understand and Adapt

Learning requires the implementation of both technology capability and organizational competency to disseminate the information. Business intelligence technology is necessary for accessing information, such as data mining and decision support tools for modeling online and offline behavior patterns. Integration of systems for transaction management among disparate applications is often critical to ensure the complete view of customer experience and the dynamics of market demand.

Learning requires an organizational approach to sharing and dissemination, facilitated by technology in some cases, but more dependent on culture and business leadership to drive the learning process.

Are new technology initiatives approached as projects to be endured for a period of time and then the organization will "return to normal"? If so, your organization may have a short lifespan. An organization's ability to reinvent itself is critical to long-term survival. A McKinsey study of 208 organizations over 18 years on their ability to succeed in the long term highlighted the critical importance of being able to change.[2] Of the 208 companies, only two survived the entire study period in their original incarnation; some failed, many merged, others changed focus.

5. Build a Balanced Approach to Deploy Capabilities

If you are considering customer relationship management as part of your enterprise technology infrastructure, taking an integrated view of your business network will improve your chances of business success.

How would you create this balanced approach? First of all, understanding that business capabilities are a combination of competency and technology enablement will broaden your company's perspective on technology implementation. By focusing on the softer skills that give life and personality to technology-enabled activity, companies will immediately understand that technology is seldom a *solution* to their business problems.

Second, develop objectives and metrics that will lead to the achievement of the business strategy. The balanced scorecard approach focuses on financial, customer, operational, and learning objectives.

6. Build a Technology Infrastructure That Is Change-Enabled

Technology standards are changing—be prepared for more change to technology infrastructure. New software and hardware are going to be necessary to add the capabilities of mobile commerce and Universal Description, Discovery and Integration (UDDI), for example. A closed technology platform that promises to do everything you need may prevent you from doing things you don't know you will need to do. Sounds like a tall order, but you need to ensure modularity of design and integration.

7. Hedge Your Bets

Demand creation is not just about new product development; it's about creating critical mass across the network of customers, partners, and allies. It's about leveraging your own resources and your extended network's resources.

New offerings are a critical part of demand creation. Sometimes, this means a new combination of services or a new combination of experiences. Accelerated delivery of service and a touch of the unexpected can enable vastly different experience, creating demand for something that is perceived as new.

If you are reading this book, it's unlikely that you dispute that modern business has entered the demand-driven economy. The customer ecosystem concept links the critical parts of business in the demand-driven economy:

◆ Ecosystem is built on experience.
◆ Experience demands adaptive strategy.
◆ Capabilities deliver adaptive strategies.

It is *technology coupled with capability* that enables each of the linkages and enables ongoing adaptation and change.

But it's not a cookie-cutter approach. Companies need to configure and customize how they will integrate with the network in ways that best leverage their assets and their network context.

Notes

1. "The New Business Technologists," Natalie Engler, *Computerworld*, November 16, 1998.
2. Charles Handy, *The Age of Paradox* (Boston: Harvard Business School Press, 1995).

Index

Bo Manning is a 20-year veteran of the technology industry and recognized leader in the CRM market, having built and led Deloitte Consulting's $500-million, market-leading CRM practice. During his tenure with Deloitte, he consulted directly with *Fortune* 1000 customers such as Charles Schwab, United Airlines, Pitney Bowes, Motorola, and Sears, and built successful alliances with leading software companies including Siebel, BroadVision, E.piphany, Vantive, and Trilogy. Prior to joining Pivotal, Manning was co-founder and CEO of Roundarch, an innovative CRM solutions company formed by Deloitte Consulting, BroadVision, and WPP Group. He has successfully led all aspects of a technology company's growth, including recruiting, product development, marketing, strategic alliances, sales, and marketing.

Chris Thorne, MBA, is Course Director of eCommerce Marketing and Strategic Market Planning at the Schulich School of Business, York University, and Senior Consultant with Advanis, Inc., a marketing strategy consulting firm specializing in demand modeling and demand strategies. Chris has a unique combination of academic, strategic, and operational perspectives on the area of customer relationship management and e-business. He is a regular contributor to *EDGE* (Executives in a Digital Global Economy) a leading Canadian publication serving executives in technology. He frequently participates as a speaker, panelist, and moderator in conferences and webcasts focusing on e-business and customer relationship management issues. He holds an MBA from York University.